LYRICAL PROTEST

MEDIA AND SOCIETY SERIES

J. Fred MacDonald, General Editor

LYRICAL PROTEST

Black Music's Struggle Against Discrimination

Mary Ellison

———————

New York
Westport, Connecticut
London

Library of Congress Cataloging-in-Publication Data

Ellison, Mary.
    Lyrical protest : Black music's struggle against discrimination /
Mary Ellison.
        p.   cm. — (Media and society series)
    Bibliography: p.
    Includes index.
    ISBN 0-275-92757-1 (alk. paper)
    1. Afro-Americans—Music—Social aspects.   2. Afro-Americans—
Civil rights.   I. Title. II. Series.
ML3556.E44   1989
782.42'1592'08996073—dc20   89-3881

Library of Congress Catalog Card Number: 89-3881
ISBN: 0-275-92757-1

First published in 1989

Praeger Publishers, One Madison Avenue, New York, NY 10010
A division of Greenwood Press, Inc.

Printed in the United States of America

∞

The paper used in this book complies with the
Permanent Paper Standard issued by the National
Information Standards Organization (Z39.48-1984).

10 9 8 7 6 5 4 3 2 1

To Karen,
who deciphered my writing and typed it wonderfully;

to Gil Scott-Heron,
who suggested this book and whose music was its inspiration;

and to my children and friends,
who sustained me through it all

Contents

Preface

This book is about black music that is sung in English and is either African or has African-American roots. Just as music in Africa accompanied and commented on every aspect of life, so African-American music has articulated emotions and responses to oppression that would otherwise have been unheard. From slavery to modern times, spirituals and then blues have given voice to the deepest personal emotions and the most intense communal fears and hopes. But the most fascinating aspect of these musics and those they spawned is that the anger they express is not contained by the music but flows out into attitudes and actions that seek to fight discrimination and unjustified aggression.

LYRICAL PROTEST

1   *Nothing but the Blues*

The coupling of black music with protest is a natural alliance. Since the first songs by black people were heard in Africa, black music has expressed resistance to oppression. Black music has also been a medium through which a whole spectrum of views about the major issues of life, as well as its day-to-day problems, can be made clear. Naturally, love and romance, sex, and the development of relationships were and are never ignored, but it is unusual to find undue attention being paid to such issues. Black music originally managed to reflect life in a very balanced way, but it is seldom appreciated that this is usually still true. People are more aware of songs that deal with romance and sometimes ignore the huge body of black music that concentrates on freedom and human rights, on equality and political possibilities, and on war and peace. Music has explored the range of human choices for black people with a lucidity and honesty rarely achieved by politicians.

Those human choices are hinted at in the music, but they are explicitly explored in the words. Consequently, this study will focus on words—on what the lyrics actually say and how the music reinforces the impact of the words. The emphasis will be placed on black music that is popular in the Western world, and only lyrics written in English will be considered. This approach has an internal consistency and coherence, since almost every branch of black popular music sung in the West is linked by a debt to the blues and, through the blues, to African music.

It is no easier to define what is meant by "black popular music" than it is to define effectively what is meant by "popular music" generally. The problem has become compounded since the late 1970s by the blurring and blending of such categories as blues, rhythm and blues, soul, funk, rap, disco, reggae, Afro-beat, and highlife. "Black music" has, in fact, become the only appropriate term for music that takes various elements from previously definable styles and genres to create new sounds.

Blues is descended in a remarkably direct way from African music. Both the musical pattern and the lyrical content are based on African models. While African music is too diversified to lend itself well to generalizations, certain characteristics are common to most of the areas from which slaves were shipped to America. Call and response, rhythmic counterpoint, polyrhythms, and melodic and harmonic sophistication are frequently encountered, as are virtuoso solo performances on instruments closely similar to the guitar and the harmonica. Even more universal are the slurred and flatted notes and melisma so characteristic of blues, and the tonal structural qualities of certain African songs are often startlingly like blues.

On the second album of *Nigeria Hausa Music* (Baren Reiter BM30L2306 and L2307) there are songs that could almost be Delta blues, while Makai from Nigeria, on *Savannah Syncopators* (BS52799), resembles, in an almost uncanny way, the eerie blues of Robert Johnson, one of the most seminally influential of the early Mississippi stylists.

Most constant of all, however, was the African musician's commitment to meaningful lyrics that reflect every human response to life, from common daily experiences to more abstract problems. During and after the slavery period, music in Africa was an integral and functional part of life, and a song was composed to enrich every occasion and emphasize every mood. Music was not only an essential means of communication but also an expression of the most fundamental feelings and facts. William Ferris, historian of the blues, commented, "African griots, slave singers, and country and urban bluesmen share a common musical tradition."[1]

That these musical and lyrical characteristics were handed down from Africa to black America is now well researched and convincingly documented by strong scholarly studies.[2] They were guarded and nurtured during slavery, emerging in work songs and hollers as well as in spirituals. Once slavery was abolished, black people lived mainly on unprofitable and unfairly administered share-cropping units, and found that freedom was accompanied by frustration and poverty. The blues crystallized in this time of hardship and disillusion. Like African music, blues simultaneously shaped and articulated community opinion. At the same time blues channeled individual expressions of sorrow and discontent, hope and humor, love and loss.

Blues seemed to spring up spontaneously throughout the South, but it was in Mississippi that it managed to enshrine the African heritage most fully. This was hardly surprising, since Mississippi had long been one of the few preponderantly black states and was notorious for harsh treatment of slaves and free blacks. Black people here had the greatest need of a culture of their own to sustain them in the face of rampant racism. In states like Tennessee the blues tradition was more influenced by European musical characteristics and the lyrics were less embittered, with only faint echoes of the dark sense of brooding menace that permeated so many Mississippi blues.

The blues that sprang from Mississippi retained the same hard edge even when they were swept north to cities like Chicago on waves of black migration. Whereas country blues complained about inequitable treatment by landlords, urban blues denounced ghetto slums and urban unemployment.

Some singers transcended their immediate situation. Robert Johnson dealt in song with issues that had a timeless, universal quality, and his lyrics were always profound and complex enough to be relevant and disturbing for people in any setting. In a different way, Bessie Smith's classic blues denunciation of poverty and exploitation has retained relevance today even though the 1920s provided a specific background.

During the 1930s the particular characteristics of the Depression and the New Deal resulted in an unusually large number of blues artists devoting themselves to commenting on or attacking the government's conservative approach to providing relief for black people and its attempt to shore up capitalism at the very time it threatened to collapse under its own weight. When the United States entered World War II, there was no shortage of blues songs assessing the significance of black people fighting for the idea of democracy—and against racism and facism—in Europe when they themselves were not afforded basic human rights at home. Once the war was over, protest became less specific and more universal in its appeal. Billie

Holiday wrote and sang "*God Bless the Child Whose Got His Own*," and created an anthem to black self-reliance and independence that would be quoted by black poets and politicians for generations to come. Though she was basically a jazz singer, she demonstrated the common roots of jazz and blues very clearly.

At the start of the twentieth century, blues combined with European instrumentation and the black art of ragtime to form jazz. Jazz was an innovative and rebellious music that usually placed only a secondary emphasis on lyrics, if they were present at all. As blues moved from rural places like Mississippi to urban areas such as Chicago, jazz elements were incorporated into the stark, often solitary sound of so many bluesmen. A reasonable-sized band, with saxophone as well as guitar or harmonica solos, became the hallmark of most rhythm-and-blues groups. By the mid-1940s the unnerving lone power of Robert Johnson, Charley Patton, or Son House had been replaced by the jauntier band sound of Muddy Waters, Big Bill Broonzy, Howlin' Wolf, and emergent rhythm-and-blues stars like Louis Jordan, Roy Brown, and Fats Domino. Rhythm and blues (in which blues were "jazzed up") was rapidly gaining a great hold on the public imagination. Many rhythm-and-blues artists had provocative political lyrics, but Louis Jordan was the master at combining humor with vociferous protest.

With rhythm and blues a transition was provided to two of the most significant musical genres of the second half of the twentieth century. Out of the fusion of a larger amount of rhythm and blues and a lesser amount of country grew rock and roll, and out of rhythm and blues and gospel (itself a development of the spirituals transformed by blues) grew soul music. Rock and roll was to bring black music and black artists into mainstream popularity just at that moment in the mid-1950s when black activists began to fight positively for civil rights. While Chuck Berry and Bo Diddley created hits with lyrics that had incisive social insight and were backed by innovative blues-based guitar riffs, Martin Luther King, Jr., was helping to organize the Montgomery, Alabama bus boycott and establish the Student Non-Violent Coordinating Committee. Just at the time black music became accepted as simply American rock and roll, black people were seeking equality as American citizens.

The struggle went on through the 1960s and 1970s, and soul music became, as blues had always been, an expression of communal black feeling and a way of raising black individual consciousness. Singers like James Brown, Nina Simone, and Aretha Franklin demanded the equality that civil rights campaigns had still not won. Gains were certainly being made, but they were never more than partial and rarely more than cosmetic. Blacks were elected congressmen and mayors at the same time that black pride and the black search for freedom were being celebrated in song. By the 1980s disillusion can be seen coexisting with hope in both the political and the musical spheres. In both areas people see progress but despair of improvement at basic economic levels. Yet black politicians still fight for real equality, and socially and politically conscious lyrics are sung by people like Gil Scott-Heron.

Even the older bluesmen continued to fight on in their music. Muddy Waters always laid himself on the line in a way that was both subtle and powerful. In his early urban blues songs "his proud declarations of dignity and intent foreshadowed the rise of Civil Rights."[3] When the movement had proved itself capable of winning only limited social and political gains, Muddy Waters was among those still ready to battle for black rights in tough, uncompromising lyrics reinforced by powerful guitar patterns.[4]

By the 1980s the musical barriers attacked in the preceding decades by innovators like Jimi Hendrix and Sly Stone had almost collapsed. Hendrix had fused blues and jazz with rock and created new experimental guitar techniques; Sly Stone had merged blues with soul and jazz and psychedelic rock, and was more responsible than anyone else for introducing funk. Stone's path-breaking music was matched by demanding and menacing lyrics that made it clear that black people would not accept mere token concessions as real change.

Funk was, in turn, a mood as much as a kind of music. "Funky," in black jargon, had always meant dirty—even smelly—and in musical terms it came to mean a sound, heavily reliant on a prominent bass line, that took in the earthiness of some of the early blues with the rhythmic fluency of jazz and some of the passion of soul. The music tends to overshadow the lyrics, but groups like George Clinton's Parliament Funkadelic frequently had lyrics that were consummately subversive.

Some of the most obviously politicized lyrics emerged from rap. Rap had always been a black street art. Black kids had for generations outtalked each other with amazing skill and proficiency, and the technique of talking over the music had been used by some early blues singers. Rapping has even been traced back to the griots of

Africa. The griots are the keepers of the history of African tribes—human repositories of facts, wit, and wisdom. When the Watts Prophets released *Rappin' Black in a White World* in 1971, their savage indictments of white injustice resulted in enormous ghetto sales. From Kurtis Blow's multiple hits to Grandmaster Flash and *The Message*, rap artists in the 1970s and 1980s compelled people to listen to the words as well as dance to the music.

Disco can be, and has been, dismissed as mindless dance music in which the words are irrelevant. To accept that is to deny the validity of the African musical heritage. African music was music to listen to and dance to, and slave music continued to have this dual function. Blues was always as much music to move the body to as stir the mind, and no one could deny the danceability of rock and roll or soul. Certainly disco has a more regular and mesmeric beat than most black music, and it can be averred that many of the lyrics are relatively insignificant, but that does not mean that disco numbers with important lyrics do not exist. Gloria Gaynor's 1979 disco hit *I Will Survive* was a strong, realistic statement about women's determination to be independent, and Grandmaster Flash and Melle Mel's 1983 disco no. 1 *White Lines* fused rap and disco to make a compelling indictment of inequality in the ghetto. The very existence of disco charts emphasizes the meaningless of terms such as "disco" to signify any particular kind of music. Numbers that rise in the disco charts are quite simply those that prove popular in discos and since all black music is basically dance music, any kind of music is likely to appear.

Black American music has become more and more impossible to slot into simple categories. The only appropriate title it is possible to give the music of someone like Gil Scott-Heron is "black music." He is, moreover, convinced that this is the only acceptable term, since breaking down the music into subsections like jazz and soul is now not only meaningless but harmful. Scott-Heron does, in fact, use elements from every branch and type of black music, weaving blues, soul, jazz, rock, rap, and funk into a coherent whole. He has always been a poet as well as a musician, and his words are crucial to his music. They make up the most impressive body of politically oriented lyrics in black American music. In a dozen albums that span a decade, Scott-Heron has attacked the corruption and hypocrisy of politics and politicians, and the dangers of nuclear power, and has forecast concerted black resistance to worldwide oppression. He is insistent that his songs be considered in relation to those of such other black activist musicians as the Isley Brothers, The O'Jays, Bob Marley, Hugh Masekela, and Fela Kuti.[5]

More recent barrier breakers convinced of the importance of black music in changing the circumstances of black people sprang from New York ghettoes. Afrikaa Bambaataa, who calls himself the Zulu ambassador from the Bronx but was born in Jamaica, uses electronic funk and rap to create great disco music with distinct political implications. He himself has said that black music

. . . was part of me growing up. Black culture gave me a lot of things and it gave the people of America strength—with message songs like "Stand" by Sly and the Family Stone, "(Say It Loud) I'm Black and I'm Proud" by James Brown, "Lord of the Land" by the Temptations. These songs gave us upliftment; to be somebody and get out there with all the Civil Rights movements. It played a strong role in my growing up. . . .[6]

A New York group urging black people to resist oppression and get to the top is Monyaka, which emerged in 1983. It originated in the West Indies, and its music is the ultimate in eclectic confusion. But it is a confusion that sounds wonderful as it happily integrates New York funk with elements of African high life and a driving core of hard-edged reggae.

Reggae has emerged since the mid-1970s as one of the most decidedly rebellious musics the world has yet known. Not surprisingly, this music evolved from a combination of rhythm and blues and indigenous African-based Jamaican music. As Saba Saakana put it: "Reggae owes its origins to the Afro-American R&B, but later expressed an identity that became associated with a specifically Jamaican musical language."[7] African survivals were strong in Jamaica, and music was no exception. African-based work songs with antiphonal call-and-response chanting had been common in slavery. By the 1950s this tradition was carried on mainly as "jamma," but it was not a music that was widely played or heard. More popular was mento, closely related to the Trinidadian calypso.

As Jamaica became more industrialized, there was a definite need for a more contemporary kind of music. That need was filled by rhythm and blues. R & B records were brought to Jamaica by migrant workers who had been cane cutting in the American South. Since radios were few and far between in the Jamaica of the 1950s, the first returning migrant workers, such as Clement Dodd, known as Coxsone, built up a "sound system" on which to play and popularize the records.[8] As transistor radios became cheaper and more widely available, the fame and popularity of rhythm and blues, and the joyous fast branch of piano blues known as boogie-woogie, spread throughout the island, but the dominance of "sound system" transmission was still unchallenged. Favorite performers were Louis Jordan, Fats Domino, and Amos Milburn.

In the late 1950s and early 1960s it became more difficult to obtain rhythm-and-blues records from the United States because they were overshadowed in record companies' order of priorities by the emergence of rock and roll and soul music. Consequently the Jamaican DJs, who had already taken to talking over many of the records, began to turn into record producers and found young Jamaicans eager to sing their homegrown kind of rhythm and blues. This up-tempo version of the blues shifted the beat and became known as ska and then as blue beat.

When the tempo was slowed somewhat in the mid-1960s, the music became known as rock steady. This was rapidly superseded by a compelling synthesis of ska and rock steady called reggae. The first reggae record, cut by Toots and The Maytals in 1967, was called *Do the Reggay*. Reggae has been called "Jamaican soul music," a sort of tropic rock and roll with accents on the second and fourth beats, a metric system so flamboyant and unique that only seasoned Jamaican drummers can keep it together and flowing.[9] Toots Hibbert said of the music, "Reggae means comin' from the people y' know? Like a everyday thing. Like from the ghetto. From majority. . . . Reggae means *regular* people who are suffering and don't have what they want."[10]

The music rapidly became Jamaica's main source of social and political commentary, but it continued to be dance music. Its political and spiritual content was accentuated by the adherence of some of the reggae musicians to the growing religion of Rastafarianism. To Rastas, living outside Africa is in itself a form of oppression, but the corruption and inequality that they see in Jamaica and in most capitalist countries makes them determined to attack the evils of "Babylon." Rastas believe firmly in the Bible and in the smoking of marijuana. They also have strict rules about appearance and food. They see Haile Selassie, emperor of Ethiopia in the 1930s, as a human manifestation of God. Their political orientation is inspired by the belief that it is a God-given duty to fight oppression and, if at all possible, to return to Africa. A Rasta hero is Marcus Garvey, a

Jamaican who won fame as a campaigner for black pride and a return to Africa in the 1920s through his U.S.-based Universal Negro Improvement Association.

The most famous of all the Rasta reggae stars is undoubtedly Bob Marley, whose powerful songs of rebellion and protest won him worldwide recognition and adulation. He denounced inequality and police harassment in riveting songs that seemed a call to action, yet Saba Saakana is convinced that he was "political only in his belief that the black man should ultimately be free."[11] It was both safer for him personally and more effective as a way of creating a world-scale impact for him to explore ways of obtaining that freedom in songs rather than in speeches. After Marley's death his manager said in a BBC2 television documentary that Marley believed in a revolution. Marcia Griffiths, one of his backup singers, The I-Threes, said in the same program that "his message was for the oppressed."[12] Marley, who had sprung from Kingston's shantytown, was giving voice to the views of people who had previously had no way of being heard.

Other members of the original Wailers, through which Marley grew to fame, also acquired impressive reputations as articulate spokesmen for oppressed black people. Peter Tosh was the most politically sophisticated, in that he saw as a clear priority the need to improve the living conditions of the poor in the city slums.[13] He wrote some of the Wailers' most memorable calls to action, including "Get up, Stand up," and in his solo career he continually demanded equal rights in song.[14]

A different and influential form of reggae emerged in Jamaica in the early 1970s. A DJ called U-Roy (Ewart Beckford) put onto disk what had for some time been a street phenomenon—he talked over records. He and a brilliant succession of DJ reggae stars made protest an elemental aspect of their sound. Closely related to the DJ "talk over" records, and even more umbilically linked to U.S. rap records, is the phenomenon of a poet talking over a heavy reggae bass line—or talking over any reggae music. Linton Kwesi Johnson's diatribes against inequality and injustice seem even more impossible to ignore than other lyrics because the poetry is spoken, not sung. The poems of the murdered Michael Smith and the very much alive and dynamic Mutabaruka explode with sardonic humor and sharp insights into the evils of corrupt governments and worldwide exploitation. Benjamin Zephaniah adds considerable sarcasm to his own particularly zany verbal demolitions of racist ideology and damaging discrimination.

Since the mid-1980s groups such as the Mighty Diamonds and the
Wailing Souls have proved that social comment and political agitation are as much a part of reggae to dance to as reggae to listen to. Joe
Higgs, a respected manager, drummer, and singer, said, "Reggae is a
music of power! Reggae meant to change the system!"[15]

Reggae has been popular in Britain ever since its inception, and in
the mid-1970s bands like Steel Pulse attracted attention because of
the juxtaposition of their danceable music and powerfully politicized
lyrics. They have since been joined by groups such as Aswad, Misty-
in-Roots, and Black Roots. The anger exploding in the songs of these
bands shows no sign of abating.

In the late 1970s reggae, ska, blue beat, and rock steady were
fundamental influences on a new type of British band. These were
bands that had mixed black and white membership, and relied for
musical inspiration on a mixture of Jamaican and black American
music. They became known as two-tone. Two-Tone was, in fact, the
name of the label on which several of these bands from Coventry
originally issued their records. Bands like The Specials and The
Selector combined fun and menace in their eclectic music and assertive lyrics. In *Ghost Town*, The Specials' 1980 no. 1 on the pop charts,
the menace seemed almost premonitory as warnings of riots coin-
cided with outbreaks of violence by black and white youths in Brixton, Bristol, Manchester and Liverpool.

Pauline Black, lead singer of The Selector, said, "The idea of
getting The Selector together was to get both black and white people
mixing at our concerts. Basically, both black and white kids have the
same problems. We want them to come together and solve them."[16]
When The Specials and The Selector split up, the groups newly
formed from the ashes, such as Fun Boy Three and Special AKA,
continued to question and attack the political and social system with
songs such as "The More I See" and "Bright Lights." Another of the
original reggae-based, radically mixed groups, The Beat, sang potent
political anthems such as "Stand Down, Margaret" and donated the
proceeds to the campaign for nuclear disarmament.

UB 40 sang equally dynamic, antiestablishment lyrics and put out
its own version of reggae songs by people like Jimmy Cliff, many of
them basically subversive. Yet they are under no illusions about the
possible impact of their songs:

To us the lyrics are secondary. It doesn't mean they're not important
because otherwise we wouldn't write them. But basically it's the music that's

important. We're a dance band. If people dance to the music but don't get into the lyrics it's cool by me. I really don't care if people aren't listening. It's nice if they are, and I get a buzz out of people listening, understanding and maybe thinking about something that hadn't occurred to them before. Maybe we've changed the minds of a few people, but it's a very small number. . . .[17]

UB 40 also feels that its racial integration reflects growing racial unity among the urban unemployed: "Generally there are lots of situations where black and white are together because they feel it's backs against the wall."[18] There are echoes here of an interview that took place in 1974 when Roebuck "Pops" Staples, of the blues- and gospel-singing Staples Singers, said, "For us it is a feeling of pride that we can help towards building a true togetherness for tomorrow."[19]

One recent phenomenon is reggae fusion bands that are composed mainly or solely of women. Women have usually played a supportive role in reggae, or have confined themselves to romantic reggae. Exceptions such as Ranking Ann and Judy Mowatt, with her brilliant *Black Woman* album, stand out as just that—exceptional. The recent explosion of female reggae bands is consequently all the more welcome. Amazulu has always had a balanced racial mix of black British, black West Indian, and white British, and was originally all women. They then added Nardo, a black male drummer, but with six women in the band the tone was definitely female. The presence of one man somehow emphasized that this was a band fighting for all kinds of integration and equality, for the human rights of all people rather than of any one subsection. They sang brilliant songs of peace and humanity, and always kept the dance beat firmly going. They believed that it is possible to shift people's opinions through lyrics that portray social and political events with more accuracy than the media, which usually have a conservative bias. They obviously did not feel that a song like the antinuclear "Greenham Time" would convert advocates of cruise missiles, but such songs could convince those already half sympathetic to the ideas expressed, or even convert those with genuinely open minds.[20] Recently they seem to have abandoned such ideals for commercial success, but their songs still linger in the mind.

The woman who was the original lead singer of Amazulu now fronts Farenji Warriors, a multiracial, multiethnic band with a woman saxophonist. They play music that draws not just on reggae but also on African highlife and Afro-beat, salsa, and soul, and produce endless hypnotic permutations. Their lyrics strongly denounce segregation and nuclear destruction, and they sing of roots that give you the strength to write and fight about what is important.[21]

The one group that is all women and all black is African Woman or Mwanamke, but, working as closely as they do with the top British reggae band, Misty-in-Roots, they are not aggressive about their feminism. More common themes are unity and harmony, though their lyrics make it quite clear that they are prepared to fight for "freedom," and that means freedom for all people, including women. Valerie Joseph, who plays lead guitar, has said that they want to show "that we as African women can write and work together even in a foreign country."[22] They play reggae but also have clear and direct African influences.

African music is a far more dominant influence in the brilliant sounds and intelligent lyrics of Orchestra Jazira, a British-based band that is made up of black African men and white British men and women. Some of Orchestra Jazira are Ghanaians, but spokesman Follo Graff says "We want no division," while Kwandotten Oteng insists that a major aim of this group is to make African music more accessible to the British public. Opata Azu adds:

We can play many kinds of music: soul, reggae . . . but they can all be found in African music. It is now time for African music to come forward. The message of that music is peace and love, and that's the kind of vibes that we want to spread around. The message of this music to the world is that music is international. We are English and Africans, and we want all Africans to realize that the time for fighting is over. It is time to unite. We are fighting against discrimination. We want Jazira to be a symbol of our unity.

Follo reinforces this:

Music is very important in getting people to investigate other cultures. Britain and America have a great responsibility in this area because they are the only real cosmopolitan places in terms of people migrating there, and in terms of culture and art going out from there, internationally.[23]

The cosmopolitan nature of music in Britain has been emphasized not only by British bands that integrate various strands of black music into a coherent whole but also by the warm reception given to African music recorded in countries such as Nigeria. The elemental appeal of African music as dance music has formed part of its attraction, but as music has become more diversified, people have developed more sophisticated responses to the dynamic complexity of African music.

Black music has formed strange and individual circles. The curve that spread from Africa to the United States and formed blues, jazz, and rhythm and blues has gone back to Africa and strongly influenced all the most vibrant elements in modern African popular music. Fela Kuti, Sunny Ade, and Ebenezer Obey lead among a plethora of popular African musicians who have created sounds that interlock twentieth-century African music with black American rhythm and blues and jazz. Fela Anikulapo Kuti is the one African musician who has had a following in the West since the late 1970s and who has consistently produced lyrics that are both in English and highly political. His music fuses African polyrhythms with rhythm and blues and jazz, and he acknowledges debts to Louis Armstrong, Miles Davies, and James Brown. Even his political ideas spring partly from the United States, since it was a black American women who introduced him to the concept of African unity, and the ideas of Malcolm X and the black radical movement in America.

Fela Kuti's Afro-beat is known as "music that inspires the revolution," and is as much a movement as a musical genre. On one album Fela used as a sleeve note an apposite quote from the Greek radical George Mangakasis: "The man dies in all who keep silent in the face of tyranny."[24] It has been said of Fela that he is "A man who is synonymous with music, and protest. Music, protest and revolt are in fact Fela's passions, the mainstays of his entire life. And as far as he is concerned, his mesmerising music is but the vehicle for an overriding social message."[25] He is one of the few musicians who has been prepared to put his life on the line for his beliefs. His house and studio have been destroyed, his women raped, and his mother and himself badly injured by government forces in Nigeria because of his beliefs. He envisages his music actually helping him to establish a government "run by the people themselves" in Nigeria. He is prepared to take his music and his political platform into the streets to campaign for such a government in the not-too-distant future.

For a man who heads a "movement of the people" and who has such a basic belief in human freedom, Fela has remarkably unprogressive views about the role of women. Obviously this can be understood only in the context of Africa, where it can be customary for women to be subservient and obedient to their husbands. Yet outside the home Fela claims he is perfectly willing for women to share freedom and political responsibility.[26] Perhaps, sometime in the future, these contradictions in his attitudes and his lyrics may be resolved, but for the moment his hatred of oppression and racism coexists uneasily with his own sexist chauvinism.

African music has remained in essence what it always was—music of and for the people, a basic form of community expression. This has been equally true of the blues; and in the blues, Archie Shepp stressed, the feelings of the community are always articulated. Shepp was convinced that Bessie Smith "could evoke in the audience a response that was *profound*, a community response from people who knew the music as she knew it, as part of their own complex history."[27] Black people have been oppressed in the United States since before blues emerged as a fully fledged musical form. Inevitably blues have become known as the music of despair, but in reality the blues transmitted hope and a stubborn determination to make the future better than the past. This was emphasized by Texas bluesman Johnny Copeland when he said, "Blues can speak for the people and to the people. Blues can make people think they can take responsibility for their own lives."[28]

As all the different forms of black music spiraled out from the blues, the best kept constant faith with the responses of people to the conditions in which they lived. Black music has never ceased to be a creative force in the raising of black consciousness.

NOTES

1. William Ferris, *Blues From the Delta* (New York: Anchor, 1979), p. 25.

2. Eileen Southern, "African Retention in Afro-American Music (U.S.A.) in the 19th Century"; David Evans, "African Elements in Twentieth Century United States Black Folk Music"; Portia Maultsby, "Africanisms Retained in the Spiritual Tradition," all in D. Heartz and B. Wadee, eds., *Report of the 12th Berkeley Congress 1977* (American Musicological Society, Barenreiter Kasel, 1981), pp. 88–98, 53–66, and 75–82, respectively; John Storm Roberts, *Black Music of Two Worlds* (London: Allen Lane, 1973), pp. 3–15, 21–22; Eileen Southern, *The Music of Black Americans: A History* (New York: W. W. Norton & Co., 1971), pp. 3–24; Marshall Stearns, *The Story of Jazz* (New York: Mentor, 1964), pp. 11–104; Paul Oliver, *Savannah Syncopators: African Retentions in the Blues* (London: Studio Vista, 1970), pp. 10–101; Olly Wilson, "The Significance

of the Relationship Between Afro-American Music and West African Music," in *Black Perspectives in Music*, 2 (1974): 3–22.

3. Gavin Martin, "Muddy Waters," *New Musical Express*, October 1, 1983, p. 28.

4. Muddy Waters, *I'm Ready,* Blue Sky/CBS, SKY 82236 (1978).

5. Interview with Gil Scott-Heron, at The Townhouse, London, April 13, 1982.

6. David Dorell, "Soul Sonicforce," *New Musical Express*, February 26, 1983.

7. Sebastian Clarke/Saba Saakana, *Jah Music: The Evolution of the Popular Jamaican Song* (London: Heinneman, 1980), Preface, 1st page.

8. Saakana, *Jah Music*, p. 58.

9. Stephen Davis and Peter Simon, *Reggae Bloodlines: In Search of the Music and Culture of Jamaica* (New York: Anchor, 1977), p. 12.

10. Davis and Simon, *Reggae*, p. 17.

11. Clarke, *Jah Music*, p. 109. See also Timothy White, *Catch a Fire: The Life of Bob Marley* (London: Elm Tree Books, 1983), p. 22.

12. "Robert Nesta Marley," BBC2 documentary, August 27, 1983.

13. Clarke, *Jah Music*, p. 111.

14. Peter Tosh, *Equal Rights*, Virgin V2081 (1977).

15. Davis and Simon, *Reggae Bloodlines*, p. 97.

16. Ethel Braite, "Talkin' Two-Tone," in *Rock Times and Top Music Special* (London: Thompson, 1981), p. 43.

17. Mat Snow, "UB 40: The Stance in Dance," *New Musical Express*, September 3, 1983.

18. Lesley White, "UB 40 Is Just a Normal Bunch of Blokes . . .," *Sounds*, March 20, 1982, p. 25.

19. J. A., "The Staple Singers," *Blues and Soul*, November 5–18, 1974.

20. Interviews with Amazulu at City of London Polytechnic, October 1, 1983, and at University of Keele, October 13, 1983.

21. Farenji Warriors Live, University of London, November 4, 1983.

22. Peter Johnson, "Woman Power," *Black Echoes*, November 19, 1983, p. 14.

23. Charles Shaar Murray, "Orchestre Manoeuvres," *New Musical Express*, March 15, 1983, p. 16.

24. Fela and the Africa 70's, *Before I Jump like a Monkey, Give Me a Banana*, Coconut, PMLP100 (1977).

25. Carlos Moore, *Fela, Fela, This Bitch of a Life* (London: Allison and Busby, 1982), p. 12.

26. Interview with Fela Kuti, Brixton, November 12, 1983.

27. Graham Lock, "Let My Notes Be Bullets," *New Musical Express*, March 5, 1983, p. 21.

28. Interview with Johnny Copeland at Dingwalls, London, July 8, 1983.

2   *Poverty: The Mark of Oppression and Exploitation*

Poverty is still endemic in most countries of the world. The majority of people in Africa, Asia, and South America live in poverty. Even in the industrialized countries of North America and Europe, poverty coexists with wealth and creates a discordant tension. In lands of plenty, people who are unemployed or paid only minimal wages live in deprivation and appalling hardship. These people are too often black, marked by color for the worst-paid jobs or no jobs at all. Frequently these black people have migrated from rural areas of bare subsistence living in the hope of finding untrammeled equal opportunities in urban industrial areas. That hope rarely materializes and new conditions are often more harsh than the old. Actual starvation has sometimes been averted by government action in countries such as the United States and Britain, but no government has yet attempted to eradicate poverty or even to diminish the existing polarities of wealth and impoverishment. These governments and those of Jamaica and most African countries may be too conscious of the threat equality would pose to the capitalist system to feel able to do anything more than make minimal cosmetic improvements and hand out limited, superficial aid.

In at least some of those countries that purport to be bastions of democracy, black people have fought for their rights as citizens of democratic societies. The concessions they have won have almost always been social and political rather than economic. Consequently, they have never yet won a power base from which to release themselves from the trap of poverty. Many black people have come to realize that such oppression is not simply a question of color. In countries like the United States, white people as well as black are exploited and poverty-stricken, but the colour of black people's skin has always made it easier for them to be identified as the ones to be kept in especially inferior positions. It is also evident that black rulers and capitalists in several African countries repress their own people as readily as the white colonialists who preceded them.

These experiences of poverty and oppression have been recounted evocatively in song. Hardship and exploitation have been explicitly decried in early Mississippi blues like "Country Farm Blues" by Son House, or far later in urban blues such as "What You Gonna Do When the Welfare Turns Its Back on You," sung by such angry interpreters such as Albert Collins and Freddie King. On *Making History*, Linton Kwesi Johnson sings of conditions in modern Jamaica:

> just people live in shack
> people livin' back to back
> 'mongst cockroach and rat,
> 'mongst dirt and disease
> subject to terrorist attack
> an' political intrigue
> constant grief an' no sign of relief.[1]

The most effective songs may be based on blues or soul, reggae or Afro-beat, funk or some new fusion, but they will always be based on real collective or individual experiences. The music that projects those experiences with intensity and power is the music that people will relate to and identify with.

Blues singer and pianist Otis Spann once said that for black people, "blues . . . is something like a book. They want to hear stories out of their own experiences, and that's the kind we tell."[2] The experiences of most black people within and outside the borders of the United States can too often be retold as stories of repression and exploitation, hunger and deprivation. For many black people such basic shared suffering is as fundamental a source of music as the universal emotions of love and hate. In a remarkably consistent way, negative experiences have produced quintessentially positive music that seems honed to a fine edge of accuracy and incisiveness. Those same experiences have also ensured that there exists in some songs a sense of communal sadness and outrage that has engendered individual mistrust of others and damagingly low self-esteem. Such songs are offset by those in which the anger is supported by black pride and rage is distilled into a desire for productive change. This kind of rage is, and often has been, directed outward at the intolerable living conditions so many black people have to endure and at the inequitable systems that produce such a disproportionately high instance of black unemployment and underemployment. As Harold Courlander wrote in 1970, for a long time "the blues have provided a convenient outlet for protest against racial injustice."[3] The blues have attacked that injustice with a unique combination of subtlety and power that has stimulated black activism without most whites even suspecting that this music was dangerous. But any music that tells the truth is dangerous, and blues have always told nothing but the truth.

Blues singers were often among the more favored members of the black community. Their music won them not only a reasonable living but also a considerable degree of respect. Yet they still sang with great frequency about "hard times," poverty, and even starvation. Most had once known poverty, and even when they had been acclaimed, some still fell on hard times. Others took seriously their roles as spokesmen for black people and feelingly described in song the deprivation they saw afflicting their neighbors in times of depression and recession, when blacks were always first fired and last hired. As Charles Keil put it, "The blues artist, in telling his story, crystallizes and synthesizes not only his own experience but the experience of his listeners."[4] Bluesmen create empathetic channels of communication between the individual and society, and give potent public voice to shared grievances and complaints. Blues, at its best, uses song to confront and face reality. Bluesmen know that their power as spokesmen for their people is real but are also aware that it is muted by the refusal of society at large to recognize that music is a force for change.

Sly Stone, who straddled blues, soul, and rock, and helped create funk, was among the black singers of the 1970s who were determined that the impact of music would not go unnoticed: "My only weapon is my singing," he said in "Poet," on the menacing revolutionary album *There's a Riot Goin' on*.[5] Bob Marley, reggae's greatest superstar of the 1970s, had an equally strong faith in the fundamental significance of music:

> All I ever had is songs of freedom
> Won't you help to sing these songs of freedom
> 'Cause all I ever had redemption songs, redemption songs.[6]

He genuinely believed it was possible to

> Emancipate yourselves from mental slavery
> None but ourselves can free our minds
>
>   . . .
>
> Won't you help to sing these songs of freedom.[7]

To Gil Scott-Heron, among the most radical of contemporary black American poets and musicians, music is the medium through which both justice and freedom can be fought for: In "Storm Music" he sings that the message the music carries "has got to be heard."[8]

Both Bob Marley and Gil Scott-Heron agree with Malcolm X that freedom is what black people are basically fighting for: "Freedom is the issue. Freedom is never given or granted—it is won." As Malcolm X said on his posthumous hit single *No Sell Out*, "If you're afraid to tell the truth, why—you don't even deserve freedom."[9] Telling the truth is one of the most singular characteristics of the best black music.

The cry for freedom, whether it was freedom from slavery or freedom from oppression and inequality, went back to the earliest days of white domination of black people. Slaves sang consistently of their hopes that freedom would come in spirituals such as "We'll Soon be Free" or

> Didn't my lord deliver Daniel, deliver
>   Daniel, deliver Daniel
> Didn't my lord deliver Daniel
>   An' why not—every man![10]

They were determined not to be diverted from their quest for freedom: "I shall, I shall not be moved."

Once slavery was ended, the first songs of the freedmen were praise songs for their emancipation.[11] Emancipation, however, provided freedom from slavery but not from oppression, inequality, or exploitation. Disillusion soon set in, and bluesmen sang songs like Memphis Slim's "Freedom."[12] Freedom remained a constant aim reiterated by Little Richard in his 1970 hit *Freedom Blues*:

> I hope that I should live to see
> When every man should know he's free
> Everybody, everybody's gonna be free. . . .[13]

He wants to bring his fellow man up today, even though "It may be very hard to do." Like Syl Johnson, he had an absolute belief in "freedom."[14] In 1975, in "Give the People What They Want," The O'Jays were in no doubt that what the people wanted was "freedom, justice and equality."[15]

Reggae stars have sung of the need for freedom throughout the 1970s and into the 1980s. In "Exodus" Bob Marley demanded: "Set the captive free."[16] And the whole of a Black Uhuru album was called *Black Sounds of Freedom*.[17] Nathalie Xavier was equally unambivalent in her 1983 single *Set Me Free*: "Set me free, I wanna go home."[18]

That songs of black people have always been about freedom is quite obvious in song poems like Gil Scott-Heron's "Bicentennial Blues" and The Last Poets' "True Blues" when blues are sung even at the point of being lynched in a symbolic bid for freedom.[19] This search for freedom through song was an overt rejection of exploitation and discrimination at all levels, and the accompanying poverty and powerlessness were continuously condemned as unfair and unacceptable.

Acceptance of oppression was never a state of mind that the majority of slaves subscribed to. Even during those constraining years of slavery, black people retained their sense of independence and individuality, and refused to be reduced to mere property. Throughout the slave period there was a ceaseless search for as much freedom as could be wrenched from an inhumane system. The ultimate goal was always total abolition of an evil institution.

Spirituals made specific appeals for freedom from enforced sale in songs like the Ashanti-style "No More Auction Block."[20] In others they seek to be

> Done with driver's driving
> Done with driver's driving
> Done with driver's driving
> Roll, Jordan, roll.[21]

Once emancipation became an imminent reality with the onset of the Civil War in 1861, songs about freedom spread like wildfire throughout the South. One of the most popular was

O Freedom, O Freedom
O Freedom over me!
Before I'll be a slave
I'll be buried in my grave,
And go home to my Lord,
And be free![22]

Once slavery was actually abolished, the slaves sang triumphantly and perhaps overoptimistically:

Free at last, free at last, I thank God I'm free at last.
Free at last, free at last, I thank God I'm free at last.

. . .

Thought my soul would rise and fly, I thank God
I'm free at last.[23]

Slavery is shown in the spirituals as a time that is marked by deprivation—not only of a physical kind but also by the lack of freedom and justice. Spirituals celebrated the existence of the "freedom train" that would not have the inequalities of the slave system of the American South:

De fare is cheap, an' all can go,
De rich an' poor are dere
No second class aboard dis train,
No difference in de fare.[24]

The poverty endemic in slavery was equally strongly attacked in a number of spirituals, such as "Poor as Lazarus, Poor as I," but bitterness is matched by hope: "I've been 'buked and I been scorned" or

Sometimes I feel like
An eagle in the air
Spread my wings an'
Fly, fly, fly.[25]

The very personal and direct deprivation of families that were broken up or threatened with being sold separately is mourned in the classic spiritual "Sometimes I Feel like a Motherless Child." Resilience in the face of hard treatment, a hallmark of slaves' response to slavery, is evident in "Hard Trials":

Sometimes I think I'm ready to drop . . .
But I thank my Lord, I do not stop.[26]

This same resilience is celebrated in more recent songs about the oppression of slavery. Bob Marley's "Redemption Song" says, for instance:

Old pirates, yes, they rob!
Sold to the merchant ships
Minutes after they took I from the
Bottomless pit
But my hand was made strong
By the hand of the Almighty
We forward in this generation triumphantly
All I ever had is songs of freedom.[27]

For Burning Spear (Winston Rodney) the memory of the "days of slavery" were filled with desperation.[28] Steel Pulse sums up the horrendous experience thus:

Slavery days
Slavery days
Slavery days
Slavery days
Oh you've been bought
Oh you've been sold
Oh cast over me
Got strung up for nothing at all
Strange fruit.[29]

Some singers of contemporary reggae see slavery as an ongoing situation that may change its image and title but retains its repressive role. The respected Jamaican group Wailing Souls denounces "Modern Slavery" and asks for freedom and humanity;[30] Black Roots, a rising Bristol band, mourns black people's "captivity" and constant lack of freedom in "What Them a Do."[31] In a similar way Lightnin' Hopkins, the brilliant Texas bluesman, sang of the hard lessons taught by slavery, lessons that made a mask of subservience an essential part of the equipment of survival.[32]

Frequently the freedom sought during and after slavery is a freedom from trouble of any kind. The classic spiritual mourns "Nobody knows the trouble I've had"[33] or, in some versions, "Nobody knows the trouble I've seen."

Another spiritual sought escape from "Trouble so Hard."[34] Perhaps it was less dangerous to talk nonspecifically about "trouble" rather than brutality or injustice, separation from family, or the endless self-evident constraints of slavery itself. At times, however, hard times and trouble are equated with quite specific hopes and disappointments:

> Hard time in ole Virginny
> Comin' in the rainbow
> Hard time in old Virginny
> Comin' in the cloud
> Hard time in ole Virginny
> My ole missus promise me
> Hard time in old Virginny
> When she die she set me free
> Hard time in ole Virginny.[35]

Once slavery ended, black people in the American South were caught in the stranglehold of an inequitable sharecropping system and emancipation came to mean here, as elsewhere, no real freedom but endless trouble. Blues singers like Maggie Jones (Faye Barnes) moaned bitterly about conditions for black people in the South:

> Goin' North, chile, where I can be free [twice]
> Where there's no hardship like in Tennessee
> Goin' where they don't have Jim Crow laws [twice]
> Don't have to work there like in Arkansas.[36]

Johnny Shines sang that he had had "trouble" all his days. It seemed to him that trouble "Gonna follow me to my grave."[37]

Bluesmen from Roy Brown through Little Milton to Phil Guy sing a traditional blues that has explored the depths of anguish and despair:

> I've got so much trouble
> Sometimes I sit and cry
> I've got so much trouble
> Sometimes I sit and cry
> But I'm gonna find my momma's grave
> Fall on the tombstone and die.[38]

In more recent times the British group Selector is typical of those who have sung of trouble that manifests itself as living a life of too little money and too few opportunities matched with a hard life full of "pressure."[39]

Most black songs were not in any way vague about trouble and hardships. Many concentrated on the common black experience of poverty. Songs sung about the inequities of the type of sharecropping established during Reconstruction in the American South stressed

> Ain't it hard to be a Nigger
> For you can't get your money when it's due

and

> Nigger makes de cotton
> De white man gets the money.[40]

Blues written in the 1920s showed that the situation hadn't changed in the intervening years:

> Seven cent cotton and forty cent meat,
> How in the world can a poor man eat?
> Flour up high and cotton down low
> How in the world can we raise the dough?[41]

A few years later Howlin' Wolf was equally bitter about the unfair rewards reaped on a Mississippi cotton sharecropping unit:

> I have ploughed so hard, baby, corns have got all in my hands
>   [twice]
> I want to tell you people, it ain't nothin' for a poor farmin' man.

Conditions for Charlie Patton on a neighboring plantation owned by Will Dockery were so bad that it seemed like a living death. Although a decade or so had passed, time and space are irrelevant when Lightnin' Hopkins sings with similar bitterness of equally inhuman exploitation on a Texas farm in "Tom Moore's Blues" or in Mississippi-based Robert Pete Williams's "Yassuh an' Wosuh Blues." Unfair imprisonment seemed an almost logical extension of the common injustice, and endless songs from Bukka White's "Parchman Farm Blues," through Sleepy John Estes's "Jailhouse Blues" to Roosevelt Charles's "Wasn't I Lucky When I Got My Time," bear sad and witty witness to such widespread inhumanity.[42]

The ultimate injustice of lynching was most classically condemned in Billie Holiday's "Strange Fruit" with all its layered allusions to "Southern trees" that "bear strange fruit" with "Black bodies swinging in the Southern breeze."[43]

Endless blues that emerged from the cities in the late and early 1930s testified to a black abhorrence of poverty as the natural order of things. As "No Dough Blues" expressed it:

> It's a hard, hard times, good man can't get no dough
> It's a hard, hard times, good man can't get no dough
> All I do for my baby don't satisfy her no mo!
>
> I ain't got no job, that's why you go'n put me down
> I ain't got no job, that's why you go'n put me down
> You gonna quit me, baby, for hard work in town
>
> Times is so hard now, maybe things will change someday
> Times is so hard now, maybe things will change someday
> If I get me a job, maybe you will change your way.[44]

"Down and Out," recorded by Kokomo Arnold, is even more direct:

> I ain't got no money
> I guess I have to rob and steal.[45]

Bessie Smith's "Poor Man's Blues" was just as threatening but was more specifically aimed at wealthy whites who were unaffected by poverty: "While livin' in your mansion, you don't know what hard times mean." She contrasts this with the starvation of working people that would "make an honest man do things you know is wrong."[46] The popularity of Bessie Smith was such that her warnings must have reached the ears of large numbers of whites as well as blacks, rich as well as poor. It is more difficult to estimate whether the effect of her words was profound or merely superficial. The fact that conditions did not change does not mean that some people were not deeply affected by the blues she sang.

Bitterness is the keynote of endless New Deal blues, from Big Bill Broonzy's despairing "Unemployment Stomp" through Blind Alfred Reed's "How Can a Poor Man Stand Such Times and Live," Speckled Red's "Welfare Blues," Bumble Bee Slims' "Hard Rocks in My Bed," Champion Jack Dupree's "FDR Blues," and Big Bill Broonzy's "WPA Blues" and "NRA Blues" to Carl Martin's cynical "Let's Have a New Deal." Blind Lemon Jefferson and Victoria

Spivey sang of crippling poverty and homeless "cold, cold nights," while Herman Johnson poured out the misery of never being able to find a job.[47] In 1936 Pete Williams implored divine intervention in "Tough Living Blues" because "Children runnin' aroun' here cryin' for bread" and "I ain't got shoes on my feet." In desperation he cried, "O Lord, I fell down on my knees, I believe I sendin' up a prayer." Robert Johnson is more typical in his sarcastic humor:

> If you cry 'bout a nickel
> You'd die 'bout a dime.[49]

There is no doubt that black people were more adversely affected by the Depression than any other group, and there is adequate evidence to show that the New Deal gave only minimal aid to those who were black and unemployed. Despite this, blues singers were aware that their plight was shared by many white people. Smokey Babe sang in a traditional Depression blues, "Hard Times Blues":

> I ain't just all alone, there is others too,
> I'm not all alone, there is others too,
> I see both white an' black walkin' the road,
> Tryin' to find somethin' to do.[50]

Others were more struck by the fact that hard times and unemployment were so prevalent in the black community that the Depression was not that different from normal.[51]

Certainly blues singers had every reason to go on bearing witness to the ongoing poverty of black people in the 1940s and 1950s. Louis Jordan directed his "Inflation Blues" and "Ration Blues" at the president and Congress while, with equal wit, Jimmy Witherspoon wrote and sang that "Money's Getting Cheaper."[52] Popular songs in the 1940s mentioned being "broke and hungry, ragged and dirty, too" and bore titles like "Starvation Blues" and "Times Is Harder Than Ever Been Before."[53] Hassled for rent and insurance, blacks sang blues like Mercy Dee and Thelma's "Rent Man Blues;" they couldn't buy food, much less pay the insurance man who sent Sonny Boy Williamson into a frenzy of despair.[54] Not only did the basic position of black people in the economy fail to improve in the 1950s but black unemployment actually doubled between 1953 and 1963. J. B. Hutto in 1954 saw the nightmare qualities of the situation: he had a dream where he was standing in a line just like the one "they had in

1929."[55] In the same year John Brim echoed Hutto's feelings and spelled out the personal consequences: to him "tough" times with no money and unpaid bills meant that, as in 1932, if you were without a job, "people you can't live happy no more."[56]

Once again, the rich are warned, this time by J. B. Lenoir, that they "better listen real deep," because when "poor people get so hungry, we gonna take some food to eat."[57] Lenoir was evidently speaking for the people on his successful single *Eisenhower Blues*, which blamed the government for prevailing poverty and unemployment.[58] This situation had not improved by the end of the 1950s, when Robert Welch sang of misery and starvation, and some people were reduced to the depths of unhappiness and dishonesty. Others sank further and, like Roy Brown, saw no further point to life itself. Brown delivered his despair over poverty that was so dreadful that suicide was the only choice, in a voice so hauntingly eerie that his voice became the vehicle for collective pain.[59]

In the 1960s as the civil rights movement that had begun in the mid-1950s gathered impetus, Ray Charles reflected the lack of economic gains by black people when he sang in "Busted" that his "bills were all due and the baby needs shoes."[60] Leadbelly, later in the decade, used the blues to mock racist hypocrisy in the "Home of the brave, land of the free," just as Leon Thomas satirized the endemic poverty in the city ghettos and called New York a city full of "fun" and "rats and roaches" and welfare and the kinds of problems that "would drive a poor man out of his mind."[61] Jimmy Dawkins, on his most riveting blues album, *All for Business*, "Never had enough of nothing."[62] Albert Collins's vision in the early 1970s was even more acerbic:

> What you gonna do
> When the weflare turns its
> Back on you
> You'll be standing out stranded
> And there ain't a thing that
> You can do.[63]

The irony of the constant poverty continuing in the ghettos while men are sent to the moon at colossal cost is satirized by Gil Scott-Heron in "Whitey on the Moon."[64] In the early 1970s Robert Shaw had nightmares in "Richard Nixon's Welfare Blues," and in *Poverty Personified* was not only hard up and hungry and too poor to pay the rent, but could not even afford to die: he got up on the point of death "because I was too poor to die."[65] Even bluesmen themselves were unusual if they escaped the trap of black poverty. Eddie Clearwater mourned his hard life and poverty, and Bobbly Bland sang that "I ain't got nothing, nothing I can call my own" and "singing for my supper is the only life I've ever known."[66]

Buddy Guy and Junior Wells were still as saddened as previous generations of bluesmen by the poverty that continued to afflict the vast majority of black people. In "Why I Sing the Blues," B. B. King pinpoints the rats and the roaches infesting the slum tenements that too many black people still call home in cities like Chicago.[67] To Albert King poverty is simply "what the blues is all about."[68]

The bleaker ranges of poverty should have been unknown to black people in the United States by the 1960s and 1970s. Such poverty was, in fact, still the normal state of affairs; but whereas blues continued to protest about the lack of funds, newly emergent soul music tended not only to express outrage at the prevalence of poverty but also to explore the power of money. Blues was never a negative psychological force, but soul accentuated the positive possibilities in a different and dynamic way. Soul acknowledged what the blues had always known—that money is the solution to at least some of life's more tedious problems. The Drifters had sung somewhat idly of "Money, Money" in the 1950s, but by 1960 the success of Motown was forecast by Barrat Strong's forceful version of Berry Gordy's song "Money."[69] The Valentine Brothers' "Money's Too Tight to Mention" (Energy 12, NRG1, 1983) was a shatteringly soulful record with tough lyrics. It had polyrhythmic bass synthesizer supporting a wonderfully emotional sax, but it never charted as high as the Simply Red cover version. When the lack of money was bemoaned by other soul singers, it was often wryly and tangentially, as when The Temptations, in their 1969 hit *Papa was a Rolling Stone* commented that when "Papa" died, all he left them was "alone."[70]

A couple of years later Stevie Wonder's brilliant "Living for the City" denounced poverty in an even more sophisticated and assured way. The message was sensational but never stentorian: only the deaf, or those who would not hear, could miss the meaning of a song that stated the impossibility of finding a job when black people are discriminated against by employers as well as by society at large.[71] The O'Jays' "For the Love of Money" was an equally cynical look at its lack in the black community.[72] To Shadee the basic need was simply to have more money. This was a raw plea from the ghetto, and all the Motown gloss, and the verve provided by a strong horn accompaniment, couldn't detract from its accuracy.[73] A decade earlier it had been enough for John Lee Hooker to say, "I need some money."[74] Now the demand was for more money, for enough to ensure a standard of living beyond mere survival.

Marvin Gaye's seminal *What's Goin' On* album, also from the early 1970s, found more cause than ever to complain about poverty. Advances in civil rights had brought no concomitant gains in economic status—work for black people was still as scarce as money, and it was disillusioning to examine "what's goin' on."[75] It seemed all the more shocking to The Temptations that in a time of affluence, black people could still be living in a one-room shack with too little to eat and no room for consideration for others deprived or stricken by poverty or segregation.[76]

The bitterness of The Temptations was matched by that of Harold Melvin and The Blue Notes, and they voiced the angry frustration of black citizens whose expectations had been falsely raised by the hope that at long last the promise of American democracy would become a reality and it would no longer be normal to see hungry children with no shelter or love to make life tolerable. They rhetorically asked where "the concern for the people" was.[77] At a time when life should have been getting better, desperation became more common than anticipation. As The O'Jays put it, life "ain't no joke" when sanity is threatened by poverty "on the bread line."[78] Stevie Wonder spelled out the full horror of the situation in more specific terms in "Village Ghetto Land":

> Families buying dog food now
> Starvation roams the streets
> Babies die before they're born
> Infected by the grief
>
> Now some folk say that we should be
> Glad for what we have
> Tell me would you be happy in Village Ghetto Land.[79]

Like Gil Scott-Heron, he sees politicians as culpable for much of the misery, in particular for delivering only false promises while not attempting to improve living conditions.[80]

The deprivation suffered by people in the black city centres during the 1970s was very real, but it was accentuated by the contrast with the lives of the wealthier segment of the white community that the media provided. It was exacerbated by the knowledge that even when compared with poor white people, black people were subject to higher unemployment, lower pay, and a lower standard of living, including education and health care, for the entire decade. The O'Jays commented acerbically on this comparative deprivation in "Rich Get Richer," pointing out that "16 families control the whole world" and make their fortunes, in part at least, from those "who live in the ghetto." They denounce the rich for always taking more than they give.[81] The Isley Brothers took this contrast between the rich and poor, the well-fed and the hungry, the powerful and the impotent, beyond the confines of the black American experience and asked when there would be "a harvest for the world" in which at least half the population always had less than they needed and those who worked hardest came home with the "least."[82] When The Last Poets attacked inequality, their intricate rhythms and dangerously truthful, accusatory political lyrics left no more room for doubt that America's dream had failed black people than did the open reference of Elaine Brown to the assassination of leading Black Panthers as "people stood by" and "waited for murders."[83]

As the 1980s ushered in the full impact of Reaganomics, black people in the United States became aware that they were not only more unemployed and underemployed than ever before, but they also had lost many of the government benefits they had received under previous administrations. Randy Crawford and The Crusaders pointed out in "Street Life" that getting old would inevitably lead to feeling "the cold."[84] To Prince Charles and The City Beat Band, lack of "Cash Money" was more acute and damaging than it had ever been.

Rappin' had been a street art for generations and had become a channel for black discontent on disk in the early 1970s with the success of The Watts Prophets' bitter political *Rappin' Black in a White World*. In the late 1970s and early 1980s rappin' on singles became a volatile and accessible way of expressing everyday frustrations. *The Message*, which topped British and American charts at the end of 1982, was a brilliant evocation of the frustrations of black life. The poverty it described was exacerbated by resentment at the affluences the American system seemed to promise. The frustration that resulted was filled with menace and a warning not to "push me 'cause I'm close to the edge."[85] It was a menace that found a more stylized echo in the brooding streetwise sounds of "In the Streets" by Prince Charles and The City Beat Band.[86]

In 1984 Curtis Mayfield, who has long been among the most articulate critics of the American dream, sang hauntingly in "Dirty Laundry" of the deprivation of Reagonomics, with its absence of work and "no weekly pay," with its fear that no one now could "trust old Uncle Sam."[87] "'Dirty Laundry' is," Stuart Cosgrove says, "a stained reality . . . a special song dedicated to the urban casualties . . . and all the children who have been scarred by life in the broken basements of the city."[88] To Lonnie Hill in 1986, too many black Americans were still unable to do what they wanted because of a pervasive lack of freedom and control as well as of money, jobs, and opportunities. He sings of these "Hard Times" (*You Got Me Running*, 10 Records Dix 38, 1986) with soulful intensity that drives home the searing sense of deprivation.

The lack of control so many black people had over basic living conditions was a focal point for songs that exploded out of studios not only in the United States but also in Jamaica, England, and Africa. The music itself provided a potent contrast with the extensive socioeconomic and political impotence of the black and the poor. Music was one area where black people could, and did, exercise a magnificent level of productive control. Black people wrote and performed words and music that could flow freely in a stream of critical comment that would never have been permitted a directly political outlet. Poverty was rejected with an uncompromising intensity that was symptomatic of a determination to try and use music to make people question the existing social order and systems of government that either condoned or were built on exploitation and oppression.

This kind of fundamental and incisive criticism was a constant preoccupation of the most arresting reggae singers. At very much the same moment in time that soul emerged as a force for change in the United States, reggae began to give Jamaican youth a channel for expressing their discontent with the poverty that constrained their lives. As early as the mid-1960s singers like Bob Andy were attacking the high unemployment and appalling conditions under the exploitative Shearer government that deprived people of a decent living with no jobs, no food, and no clothes.[89] Michael Manley promised release from suffering and cast himself as the people's redeemer, but once he was elected prime minister, hope was replaced by hardship as great as any the poor of Jamaica had ever known.

Bob Marley and the Wailers rapidly denounced the conditions in the Kingston ghetto as a "Concrete Jungle," and Boston Jack sang bitterly of "Starvation."[90] Bob Marley and the Wailers themselves had "suffered" in the ghetto, and this experience had engendered in Marley "a social analysis marked with vigorous protest against oppression." He became known as the "Ambassador of the Oppressed."[91] He gave ultimate expression to the hunger that could well feed violence:

> Them belly full but we hungry
> A hungry mob is an angry mob.[92]

The extremes of poverty and wealth that continued to exist in Jamaica under Manley, who had committed himself to a more egalitarian society, combined with the impact of Rastafarianism to make many reggae singers reject capitalism entirely. I-Roy condemned the exploitation that now seemed inherent in a capitalist society. In "Sufferer's Psalm" he transformed the words and meaning of the 23rd Psalm into a hymn for poor people that began "If the capitalist is our shepherd, we will always want."[93]

Tapper Zukie also saw the ghetto as exploited and discriminated against, with children getting inadequate education and people living in slum conditions.[94] At much the same time, during the ongoing disillusionment of the late 1970s, The Royals sang with anger, as well as subtlety, power and precision, on the album *Pick up the Pieces*, one of the greatest slices of Jamaican music ever. With numbers such as "Sufferer of the Ghetto," Roy Cousins painted impassioned sound pictures of destitution and pain that managed to be both tangible and elusively universal.[95] Equally persuasive and convincing were The Ethiopians' reflective denunciation of harassment on *Slave Call* and Third World's adventurous, eclectic, and polyrhythmic rejection of oppression, *96° in the Shade*.[96]

Horace Andy sang with assured and contained rage of what it was like to "Live in the City" in involuntary deprivation, and Papa Michigan and General Saint pushed for black people to organize their way out of the ghetto and the "Downpression" such circumstances engendered.[97] In "Trench Town" and "Ambush," Bob Marley was astute enough to denounce the casuistry that seemed to say that poverty and underprivilege were in some way deserved, rather than part of an abhorrent system that would keep poor people in chains and deny them their birthright of freedom: "Every time they can reach us" through political chicanery, "They keep us hungry.[98] In "Survival" he again attacked hypocrisy and the polarization of wealth where some people "got everything" and "some people got nothing."[99]

Wailing Souls similarly exposed the exploitation of "modern, modern slavery," while Jean Adebambo gave vent to her anger about the *Hardships of Life*, and Barbara "Lady Ann" Smith compared the "pain" of slavery with the way black people were still treated as subhuman.[100] In 1987, Countryman is among the numerous bands that still find it necessary to attack the inhumanity of ghetto living ("Poor Me Natty Dread," MT Music, 1987).

Peter Tosh was once unique among the earlier reggae stars in that he saw "improving the condition of the urban poor" as "an absolute priority." Before 20,000 people at the Peace Concert of 1978 he attacked the democracy of Manley's Jamaica as "just a shitstem layed down to belittle the poor."[101] Less pointed but still obviously condemnatory of both the prevailing poverty and the politicians who sanctioned it were contemporary songs that emerged from international reggae stars such as The Mighty Diamonds, Sugar Minott, Jimmy Lindsay, Bunny Wailer, Gregory Isaacs, and Jimmy Cliff.[102] The popular Jamaican group Black Uhuru explained at this point in time (1984) "It was necessary to reflect the poverty and the entire livity to bring about a certain level of consciousness."[103] That consciousness was further raised by the pointed comments and directives of such widely followed DJs as Tapper Zukie, I-Roy, and Jazzbo. Jazzbo explicitly condemned the capitalism that exploited the poor and chanted, "I want socialist."[104]

There are strong links between the DJs and the reggae dub poets. It would be difficult to find records that center more solidly on the evils of capitalist oppression than those of Mutabaruka, Michael Smith, and British-based Linton Kwesi Johnson and Benjamin Zephaniah. On albums such as Mutabaruka's *Check It*; Michael Smith's *Mi Cyaan Believe It*; Linton Kwesi Johnson's *Dread, Beat and Blood*, *Bass Culture*, *Forces of Victory*, and *Making History*; and extended singles such as Benjamin Zephaniah's *Dub Ranting*, there is a furious anger that is focused closely on the unacceptability of the oppression and poverty assigned to black people by Western society.

Mutabaruka powerfully declaims that "De system is a grave. The system, the system is a fraud," while Michael Smith has said he was directly inspired by the inequities inherent in his surroundings: "the contradiction in the system . . . the bad housing."[105]

Poverty and racism have always preoccupied the uncompromising poems of Linton Kwesi Johnson, and he has condemned the racism that manifests itself through the National Front or victimization in Bradford. On his album, *Making History* he directs his attention to the crucial question "What About di Working Class?"[106] In an interview for *Black Music* he explains that for the people who are poor, "liberation from human suffering and oppression" is by far the most important issue.[107] Similarly, to Benjamin Zephaniah, while everybody wants peace, "Peace to me is to do with social equality and even employment. . . . Social justice . . . this is the struggle you can't give up, no matter what."[108] On record he attacks with a direct precision the social inequality of the "fascist" regimes of Ronald Reagan and Margaret Thatcher. He rants at a more personal level that "Dis policeman is kicking me to death,"[109] to the accompaniment of hypnotically rhythmic music. Mutabaruka came to the conclusion on *Check It* that black men were doomed if they continued to allow themselves to be the victims of such racism.

Conditions for too many black people in Britain had been marked by poverty and discrimination long before the emergence of the dub poets. This was always reflected in music but was given especially cogent articulation when reggae became a major musical force. Early British reggae groups like Matumbi edged their way toward the more open denunciation of racism that characterized groups such as Steel Pulse in the 1970s. On albums like *Handsworth Revolution* and *Tribute to the Martyrs*, positive, ebullient rhythms were matched by carefully crafted lyrics that unpicked the seams of blatant, damaging prejudice. Few more powerful tracks than "Ku Klux Klan" have been laid down by a British reggae band.[110] In 1982 Steel Pulse chose the ironic title *True Democracy* to attack a system that seemed nothing more than a hollow fantasy in which police harassment was more of a day-to-day reality than any democratic idea.[111] On *Earth Crisis*, in 1984, David Hinds showed he could widen his vision to encompass a thoughtful evaluation of worldwide oppression.[112]

Merger was another British reggae band that attempted to expand the music and expound the truth. *Exiles* in 1978, said guitarist Barry Ford, was the story

. . . of the plight of black people in Britain. We start with '77, the base. It's about the time we're in now. Jubilee year and people living in poverty and fear. . . . Then we go down to "Ghetto Child." And black community in any city in the world. And it don't necessarily apply only to black people. . . . if you go to Newcastle you see the same thing we got in Brixton, working class people who haven't got no food, haven't got no clothes, living in a nightmare.[113]

Less than a year later the formerly rather bland Cimarons released the hardest-hitting of antiracist singles, *Rock Against Racism*, on which the heavy rhythm matched the weight of the lyrics.[114] It reinforced the impact of Steel Pulse's magnificent attack on racism in the same year and led some people toward the less accessible Rasta chant of Blazing Son's *Chant Down the National Front*.[115] Simultaneously Aswad was evolving into a group that was to have no equal when it came to delivering storming onslaughts on the poverty and racism shockingly prevalent in Britain in the late 1970s and early 1980s. As lead singer Brinsley Ford said, "Racism is based on ignorance. . . . And that ignorance and fear is being instilled into the people by the leading members of society, see? . . . So with racism you have to look further than just racism, it's the system that determines such things."[116] Aswad has always tried to make people ask questions about the circumstances in which they live and become aware that poverty is not disconnected from political decisions, and can be solved only by political solutions.

Aswad and Misty-in-Roots are among the many British reggae bands that have sought to raise levels of consciousness about the interaction of politics and deprivation as well as politics and racism on albums such as Aswad's *Live and Direct* and Misty-in-Roots' *Wise and Foolish*.[117] Misty-in-Roots has denounced the corruption of capitalism on singles such as *Poor and Needy* and on a compilation album with other relatively new groups seeking change, such as Abacush and African Women.[118] These bands are London-based, but London has no monopoly on new reggae talent. Bands like Black Roots from Bristol and Jah Warriors from Ipswich make bitingly truthful albums about poverty and inequality.[119]

Individual singers are no less outraged by poverty than groups; on *Down in the Ghetto*, Sister Carol condemns black deprivation in sharply aware lyrics.[120] Winston Reedy is only one among the many male reggae stars who in songs like "Message to Father" is impassioned in his denunciation of a world oblivious to the sufferings of those without enough basic necessities to feed the body, much less free the spirit.[121] Smiley Culture, Asher Senator, and Papa Levi are three of the new British-based DJs whose rantings are filled with attacks on unemployment.

Since the late 1980s British music has been regenerated by an infusion of sounds that mix musical traditions and ethnic personnel. Bands like The Specials and Selector from Coventry, UB 40 and The Beat from Birmingham, and, more recently, Restriction from Bristol have, or had, black and white members and multifaceted sounds. The Specials wrapped ska, blue beat, reggae, and soul in storming rock and roll. The five whites and two blacks sang of the deprivation that was endemic among British youth. "Concrete Jungle" channeled anger at obscene living conditions into a sound that was relentless but free, economical but musically dense and inventive.[122] Selector more specifically mourned the lack of money in "Deep Water."[123]

UB 40 put a similar dilemma even more eloquently when it laid down the position of the unemployed masses to a persistent reggae rhythm; using the fact that one person in ten was unemployed in Britain in the early 1980s: "A statistical reminder of a world that doesn't care."[124] Unemployment was not just an amorphous cause to UB 40. Half of the group had been on the dole, and all of them had been born into impoverished circumstances. They knew from friends and acquaintances, if not from personal experience, that poverty could lead to crime: "Poverty has turned him to crime," and anyone without work became a "prisoner in the land of the free."[125]

In 1984 Special AKA not only demanded the freedom of Nelson Mandela on *Free Nelson Mandela*, but also found humor in the bitterness of being on the dole in "Bright Lights."[126] Simultaneously Sade has asked the question that could tumble out from any of over three million British unemployed: *When Am I Going to Make a Living*. As the song spills out, barbs coated in velvet sound an indomitable spirit celebrating a refusal to "give in" or give up.[127]

Sade Adu is half Nigerian. It is a Nigerian singer and musician who has most dangerously denounced poverty both internationally and within the confines of his country as a consequence of elitist and undemocratic forms of capitalism. In 1976 on *Upside Down*, Fela Kuti attacked the Gowon-Obasajo government in Nigeria for creating endless jobless beggars who are "hungry every day." Through music, he felt, the eyes of the oppressed could be opened and the anger of the deprived be unleashed.[128]

Fela Kuti is one of the few singers who has consciously put his body where his mouth is, and he has been challenged for his temerity. Maybe he thought the risks he was taking when he criticized the Nigerian government were unlikely to lead to any personal harm. He said: "I'm just a musician, a crazy artist saying a lot of crazy things. And then they take a look at what I stand for—nationalism, Pan-Africanism, anti-colonialism. These are things they stand for. So if they come down on me, they would be coming down on themselves."[129] He was wrong—a few days after these words were spoken in February 1977, his house was raided, and he and his wives and mother were attacked by government forces. He and his mother were badly injured; his mother never fully recovered before she died. Fela has not regained the strength in one of his arms. His wives were raped and beaten. An investigative tribunal warned of the repercussions of subversion, and Fela received no compensation. Indeed, his music was temporarily banned on the radio in Nigeria. This did not prevent Fela from releasing two albums in 1977 and 1979 dedicated to those who were beaten, raped, and tortured during the horrendous attacks on Kalakuta, his wrecked home.[130] Uncrushed, he continued to denounce corrupt government and the oppression of the people in live shows and on albums such as *Black President* and *Original Sufferhead*.[131] Since 1979 Fela has been a threat rather than a critic because he has sought actual political power. He plans to use his music to be elected president. Moreoever, he wants to use music to undermine the oppressive political system by returning power to the people.[132] Time will tell if this is more than a fantasy, if music can have real political impact of that magnitude.

There are other African musicians who have openly protested unacceptable political constraints and poverty: Thomas Mapfumo, Sonny Okosun, and Mohammed Malcolm Benn. That there are not more is perhaps accounted for by Les Quatres Etoiles's explanation of the lack of protest in Zaire: "The reason for this is because if performers were to use the media to protest against the country's dictator, they and their kin would meet a violent fate."[133]

Despite sounds and lyrics that in South Africa would "doubtless [be] considered criminally political,"[134] Hugh Masekela has avoided such a fate by remaining in exile from his homeland. Years of living in America and playing with American musicians have in no way defused his anger about the humiliation and bare subsistence that are common for black people in South Africa. On albums like *Masekela*,

Colonial Man, and *The Boy's Doin' It*, the anger poured out, sustained and strengthened by a golden arc of trumpet virtuosity. More recently Masekela has played in London's Crystal Palace Bowl in aid of freeing Nelson Mandela and has acquired a permanent base in Botswana, just over the border from South Africa. While he still fights political oppression with his own music, his more recent albums, such as *Techno-Bush*, provide opportunities for South African youth to escape oppression and explore their own talents in his mobile studio.[135]

Also regarded as subversive—but not subversive enough to be driven into exile, as were not only Hugh Masekela but also myriad other black musicians, such as the talented Julian Bahula—was Juluka. Juluka was unusual in being a band that was Zulu inspired and contained black and white members. Its hit single *Scatterlings of Africa* did not directly attack the South African system but highlighted the situation that system imposed on many who lived within its authority, uprooted and homeless and increasingly hostile.[136]

Successful black singers of songs in English do not confine their concern to their own countries. Frequently they link exploitation of their own people with that of repressed groups throughout the world. It seems to be in this spirit that Peter Tosh was so strong in his support for the Palestinians' battle for their lost homeland. Gil Scott-Heron and Mutabaruka are appalled by the intolerable and demeaning South African system of apartheid. To Mutabaruka, if South Africa was "not free," neither could he or anyone else be free.[137] Gil Scott-Heron sees links in the racism that blights black lives in *From South Carolina to South Africa*.[138] Jimmy Cliff has felt his radicalism being reawakened by travels through Africa; his exposure to the plight of "the struggling and the dispossessed" has hardened his determination to expose injustice in his music. "I sing about truths!" he insisted in a 1984 interview, "So long as the rich won't share with the poor and so long as youth is raised just to die in war, I, Cliff, will keep on."[139]

The fact that most young black people are still raised in ghettos is the theme of "Children of the Ghetto," written by Chris and Eddie Amoo, and recorded by their band, The Real Thing. It is one of the most frequently cut numbers of recent times. Among the most significant versions are those of Philip Bailey and Courtney Pine.[140] The variations in musical styles range from funk to jazz, and all emphasize different undesirable aspects of being a child in a black ghetto. All use diverse musical effects to reinforce the tragic impact of this urban disaster. Possibly most effective is Courtney Pine's mournful saxophone, which reluctantly bears continuing witness to a phenomenon whose demise should have been celebrated long ago.

When songs are sung about oppression, whether it is channeled through racism, poverty, or brutality, they are elementally dangerous because they are exposing the reality of situations that those in power would prefer to be masked. Songs that strip away illusions and show things as they are, are subversive simply because they tell the truth. In societies structured around discrimination, nothing is more subversive than the truth.

NOTES

1. Son House, "Country Farm Blues," *The Legendary Son House 1941–1942*, Roots RSE 1; Albert Collins, *Ice Pickin'*, Sonet SNTF 707 (1978); Freddie King, *All His Hits*, Federal Bid 8012 (1977); Linton Kwesi Johnson, "Reggae Fi Dada," *Making History*, Island/ILPS 9770 (1984).

2. Peter Welding, sleeve note to Otis Spann's *Chicago Blues: Nobody Knows My Troubles*, Polydor 545030.

3. Harold Courlander, *Negro Folk Music, U.S.A.* (New York: Columbia University Press, 1970), p. 136.

4. Charles Keil, *Urban Blues* (Chicago: University of Chicago Press, 1970), p. 161; see also Harry Oster, *Living Country Blues* (New York: Minerva Press, 1975), p. 59.

5. Sly and the Family Stone, *There's a Riot Goin' On*, Epic EPC 64613.

6. Bob Marley and The Wailers, "Redemption Song," *Uprising*, Island ILPS 9596 (1980).

7. Marley, "Redemption Song."

8. Gil Scott-Heron, *Reflections*, Aristo/Spart 1180 (1982).

9. Malcolm X with Keith Le Blanc, *No Sell Out*, Tommy Boy TB 840 (1983).

10. John Lovell, Jr., *Black Song: The Forge and the Flame: The Story of How the African-American Spiritual Was Hammered out* (New York: Macmillan, 1972), pp. 331, 329.

11. Lovell, *Black Song*, p. 331.

12. Memphis Slim, *Right Now*, Trip TLP 8025 (1972).

13. Little Richard, *This Is Little Richard*, Reprise RS 6406 (1970).

14. S. Johnson, *Is It Because I'm Black*, Twinight LPs 1002.

15. O'Jays, "Survival," *Philadelphia*, PIR 80765 (1975).

16. Bob Marley and The Wailers, *Exodus*, Island ILPS 9498 (1977).

17. Black Uhuru, *Black Sounds of Freedom*, Greensleeves GRE1 23 (1981).

18. Nathalie Xavier, *Set Me Free*, People Unite Musicians Cooperative, P.U./NAT 001 45 12in. (1983).

19. Gil Scott-Heron, *The Mind of Gil Scott-Heron*, Arista AL 8301 (1978); The Last Poets, *Jazzoetry*, Douglas SDLP 6001 (1976).

20. John Storm Roberts, *Black Music of Two Worlds* (London: Allen Lane, 1973), p. 168.

21. Roberts, *Two Worlds*, p. 173.

22. Henry H. Krehbiel, *Afro-American Folk Songs* (New York: Schirmer, 1914), p. 21.

23. Lovell, *Black Song*, p. 331.

24. Lovell, *Black Song*, p. 333.

25. Lovell, *Black Song*, pp. 340, 233.

26. Lovell, *Black Song*, pp. 298, 323.

27. Bob Marley and the Wailers, *Uprising*, Island ILPS 9596 (1980).

28. Burning Spear, *Live*, Island ILPS 9513 (1978).

29. Steel Pulse, "Bad Man," *Handsworth Revolution*, Island ILPS 9502 (1978).

30. Wailing Souls, *Inchpinchers*, Greensleeves GREL 47 (1983).

31. Black Roots, *Black Roots*, Kick KK LP02 (1983).

32. Lightnin' Hopkins, "Slavery," *The Texas Bluesman*, Arhoolie F 1034 (1967).

33. Miles Mark Fisher, *Negro Slave Songs in the United States* (New York: Russell and Russell, 1968), p. 94.

34. Vera Hall, "Troubles So Hard," *Sounds of the South: The Classic Alan Lomax Sessions*, Atlantic 590033.

35. Lydia Parrish, *Slave Songs of the Georgia Sea Islands* (New York: Creative Age Press, 1942), p. 234.

36. Maggie Jones, "North Bound Blues," in D. Stewart-Baxter, *Ma Rainey and the Classic Blues Singers* (London: Studio Vista, 1976).

37. Johnny Shines, "Troubles All I See," *Too Wet to Plow*, Blue Labor, BL 110 (1977).

38. Little Milton, "Hard Luck Blues," *Blues 'n' Soul*, STS 5514 (1974).

39. Selector, "Too Much Pressure," *Dance Craze: The Best of British Ska Live!* Chrysalis/Two Tone CHR 1299 (1981).

40. Edna Edet, "One Hundred Years of Black Protest Music," *Black Scholar*, 7, no. 10 (July–August 1976): 43, 41.

41. Bob Miller, "Seven Cent Cotton and Forty Cent Meat," in Alan Lomax, Woody Guthrie, and Pete Seeger, eds., *Hard Hitting Songs for Hard-Hit People* (New York: Oak Publications, 1967), p. 38.

42. Mike Leadbitter, *Delta Country Blues* (Bexhill-on-Sea: Blues Unlimited Publications, 1968), p. 9; Jeff Todd Titon, *Early Downhome Blues: A Musical and Cultural Analysis* (Urbana: University of Illinois Press, 1977), p. 6; Charlie Patton, *Founder of the Delta Blues*, Yazoo

L-1020; Lightnin' Hopkins, "Tom Moore Blues," *The Texas Bluesman*, Arhooli F 1034 (1967); Bukka White, *Mississippi Blues*, Sonet SNTF 609; *Sleepy John Estes 1929–1940*, Asch RFF8; Oster, *Living Country Blues*, pp. 331–32, 138–42. See also Roosevelt Charles, *Mean Trouble Blues*, RYE VRS 9136 (1964).

43. Billie Holiday, *The Voice of Jazz*, Vol. I, Verve 2304 104.

44. Blind Blake, *No Dough Blues*, Paramount 12723-B.

45. Kokomo Arnold, "Down and Out," in Lomax, et al., eds., *Hard Hitting Songs*, p. 50.

46. Bessie Smith, "Poor Man's Blues," *Empty Bed Blues*, CBS 66273.

47. Big Bill Broonzy, *Unemployment Stomp*, Vocalion 04378; Speckled Red, *Welfare Blues*, Bluebird 8069A; Carl Martin, "Let's Have a New Deal," *Blues Classics*, no. IV; Bumble Bee Slim, *Hard Rocks in My Bed*, Vocalion 03328 (C1229-1); Blind Lemon Jefferson, *One Dime Blues*, Paramount 12578-B; Victoria Spivey, "Detroit Man," *Victoria Spivey Recorded Legacy of the Blues*, Spivey Reissues LP 2001; Herman Johnson, "Depression Blues," in Oster, *Living Country Blues*, p. 48.

48. Oster, *Living Country Blues*, pp. 199–200.

49. Robert Johnson, "Fair Deal Gone Down," *King of the Delta Blues Singers*, BS 62456.

50. Robert Brown (Smokey Babe), "Hard Time Blues, *Country Negro Jam Sessions*, Folk Lyric Records FL 111 (1960).

51. Paul Fryer, "Can You Blame the Colored Man?" The Topical Song in Black American Popular Music," *Popular Music and Society* 8, no. 1 (1981): 21.

52. Louis Jordan, "Inflation Blues," *Choo Choo Ch' Boogie*, MFP 50557, and *Ration Blues*, Decca 8654; Jimmy Witherspoon, "Money's Getting Cheaper," *Ain't Nobody's Business!* Black Lion BLP 30147.

53. Stefan Grossman, *Delta Blues Guitar* (London: Oak, 1969), pp. 105, 113; Lomax et al., eds., *Hard Hitting Songs,* p. 59.

54. *City Blues*, Specialty SNTF 5015; Blind Derby, "Meat and Bread Blues," *Savannah Syncopators*, CBS 52799; Sonny Boy Williamson, *Insurance Man Blues*, Bluebird B8034.

55. J. B. Hutto, *Things Are So Slow*, Chance 1165.

56. John Brim, "Tough Times," Elmor James and John Brim, *Whose Muddy Shoes*, Chess CXMP2007.

57. J. B. Lenoir, *Everybody Wants to Know*, Chess 410 (1955).

58. J. B. Lenoir, *Eisenhower Blues*, Parrot 862 (1955).

59. Oster, *Living Country Blues*, p. 201; Roy Brown, "Hard Luck Blues," *Hard Luck Blues*, Gusto KS 1130 (1976).

60. Ray Charles, *Recipe for Sound*, ABC ABCS 465.

61. Leadbelly (Huddie Leadbetter), *Bourgeoisie Blues*, Ember W132 (1959); Roberts, *Black Music*, pp. 193–94.

62. Jimmy Dawkins, *All for Business*, Delmark DS 634 (1973).

63. Albert Collins, "When the Welfare Turns Its Back on You," *Ice-Pickin'*, Sonet SNTF 707 (1978).

64. Gil Scott-Heron, *The Revolution Will Not Be Televised*, Flying Dutchman TCA SF8428 (1978).

65. Robert Shaw, *Born in Texas*, Xtra 1132 (1972), and *Poverty Personified*, BDL 10613 (1975).

66. Eddie Clearwater, *Two Times Nine*, Charly R&B CBR 1025; Bobby Bland, "Sittin' on a Poor Man's Throne," *Reflections in Blue*, ABC BLL 5196 (1977).

67. B. B. King, "Why I Sing the Blues," *Best of B. B. King*, ABC XQ-767 (1973).

68. Albert King, *I Wanna Get Funky*, Stax STD 5505 (1974).

69. Barratt Strong, *Money*, Anna 1111 (1960).

70. The Temptations, *Papa Was a Rollin' Stone*, Gordy 7121 (1972).

71. Stevie Wonder, "Living for the City," *Intervisions*, EMI STMA 8011 (1973).

72. O'Jays, *For the Love of Money*, Philadelphia International 3544 (1974).

73. Shadee, *I Just Need More Money*, Tamla T7-368RI (1979).

74. John Lee Hooker, *Blue!*, Fontana FLJ119 (1960).

75. Marvin Gaye, *What's Goin' On*, Tamla Motown STML 11190 (1971).

76. The Temptations, "Cloud Nine" and "Ball of Confusion," *The Temptations*, Motown Special STXM 6002 (1970).

77. Harold Melvin and The Blue Notes, "Where's the Concern for the People," *Now Is the Time*, ABC AA 1041 (1977).

78. O'Jays, "Survival," *Survival*, Philadelphia International PIR 80765 (1975).

79. Stevie Wonder, "Village Ghetto Land," *Songs in the Key of Life*, Motown TMSP 6002 (1976).

80. Stevie Wonder, "He's Mista Know It All," *Innervisions*, EMI STMA 8011 (1973) and "You Haven't Done Nothing," *Fulfillingness First Finale*, Tamla IM46022 (1974).

81. The O'Jays, *Survival*, Philadelphia International PIR 80765 (1975).

82. Isley Brothers, "Harvest for the World," *Forever Gold*, CBS/TNECK 34452 (1977).

83. The Last Poets, *The Last Poets*, Celluloid CAL 208; Elaine Brown, "And All Stoody By," *Seize the Time*, Vault 131 (1970).

84. The Crusaders, "Street Life," *Fingers Off*, Louis PBR80 20 (1982).

85. Prince Charles and The City Beat Band, *Combat Zone*, Virgin V2298 (1984); Grandmaster Flash and The Furious Five, *The Message*, Sugar Hill SHL 117 (1982).

86. Prince Charles and The City Beat Band, *Gang War*, Platinum GRP LP 101 (1983).

87. Curtis Mayfield, "Dirty Laundry in the Country," *Honesty*, Epic EPC 25317 (1983).

88. Stuart Cosgrove, "Songs in the Key of Life: Interview with Curtis Mayfield," *Echoes*, February 25, 1984.

89. Patrick Hylton, "The Politics of Caribbean Music," *Black Scholar*, September 1975, p. 28.

90. *Soul of Jamaica*, Island HGLP 15 (1973).

91. Hazel Reid, "Bob Marley: Up from Babylon," *Freedomways*, Third Quarter 1981, pp. 177, 172.

92. Bob Marley and The Wailers, "Them Belly Full (But We Hungry)," *Natty Dread*, Island ILPS 9281 (1974).

93. I-Roy, *Truths and Rights*, Grounation GROL 54 (1976).

94. Tapper Zukie, "Ghetto Rock," *Peace in the Arena*, Virgin F-2 1009 (1978).

95. The Royals, *Pick up the Pieces*, Magnum DGAD 1004 (1978); Curtis May, "Album of the Month, Reviews: Reggae Albums," *Black Music*, Februrary 1978, p. 49.

96. The Ethiopians, *Slave Call*, Third World and WS 15 (1977); Third World, *96° in the Shade*, Island ILPS 9443 (1977).

97. Horace Andy, *Exclusively*, Solid Groove SGL 107; Papa Michigan and General Saint, *Downpression*, Greensleeves GRE1 42.

98. Bob Marley, *Confrontation*, Island/Tuff Gong ILPS 9760 (1983).

99. Bob Marley, *Survival*, Island ILPS 95421 (1979).

100. Wailing Souls, *Inchpinchers*, Greensleeves GREL 47 (1983); Jean Adebambo, *Hardships of Life*, Ade J10AJ103 (1982); Barbara "Lady Ann" Smith, *Informer*, Joe Gibbs Music JGM 1-60074 (1983).

101. Sebastian Clarke (Saba Saakana), *Jah Music* (London: Heinemann, 1980), pp. 111–12.

102. The Mighty Diamonds, *Deeper Roots*, Frontline FL 06001; Sugar Minott, *Ghettoology*, Trojan TRLS 173; Jimmy Cliff, *In Concert,* Rep MS-2256, and "The Harder They Come," *Reggae Greats*, Island IR 414 (1985); Gregory Isaacs, *Soon Forward*, Frontline FL 1004.

103. P. Bradshaw, "The Bright Soul," *New Musical Express*, January 14, 1984, p. 67; Jack Barron, International Anthems, *Sounds*, July 7, 1984, p. 27.

104. Clarke, *Jah Music*, pp. 123–24.

105. Mutabaruka, *Check It!*, Alligator AL 8306 (1983), and "Live: Tribute to Michael Smith 1954–83," *New Musical Express*, November 26, 1983, p. 38; Paul Bradshaw, "Dub Poet Michael Smith Murdered," *New Musical Express*, August 27, 1983, p. 2.

106. Linton Kwesi Johnson, *Dread Bet and Blood*, Virgin VX 1002 (1978); Linton Kwesi Johnson, *Making History*, Island ILPS 9770 (1984).

107. Dotun Adebayo, "The Alternative History Man," *Black Music and Jazz Review*, March 1984, p. 15.

108. Mark Kemba, "Dub Poetry in Motion," *Black Echoes*, July 30, 1983, p. 10.

109. Benjamin Zephaniah, "I Don't Like," *Dub Ranting*, Radical Wallpaper Rad Wall 005 (1983).

110. Steel Pulse, *Handsworth Revolution*, Island ILPS 9502 (1978); see also Steel Pulse, *Tribute to the Martyrs*, Island ILPS 9568 (1979).

111. Steel Pulse, *True Democracy*, Wiseman Doctrine WMDLP 001 (1982).

112. Imruh Bakari Caesar, "Pulse Points," *Echoes*, March 10, 1984, p. 10.

113. Chris May, "Merger: The New Breed," *Black Music*, February 1978, p. 13.

114. The Cimarons, *Rock Against Racism*, Polydor 12in CIMA 12 (1979).

115. Blazing Sons, *Chant Down the National Front*, Cool Ghoul COOL 002 (1979).

116. Jack Barron, "Lion Taming," *Sounds*, January 7, 1984, p. 9.

117. Aswad, *Live and Direct*, Island IMA6 (1983); Misty-in-Roots, *Wise and Foolish*, People Unite, PU 101.

118. Misty-in-Roots, *Poor and Needy*, People Unite (1983); Misty-in-Roots with Abacush, African Women, et al., *In Progress*, People Unite PU 104 (1984).

119. Black Roots, *Black Roots*, Kick KICLP 02 (1984); Jah Warriors, *Poor Man's Story*, Vista (1984).

120. Sister Carol, *Down in the Ghetto*, Jah Life (1984).

121. Winston Reedy, "Message to Father," *Dim the Light*, Inner Light IN 001 (1983).

122. The Specials, "Concrete Jungle," *The Specials*, Two Tone/Chrysalis CDL JT 5001 (1979).

123. Selector, "Deep Water," *Celebrate the Bullet*, Chrysalis CHR 1306 (1981).

124. UB 40, "One in Ten," *Present Arms*, International LP DEP4 (1983).

125. UB 40, "The Prisoner," *UB 40*, International LP DEP3 (1982).

126. Special AKA, *Free Nelson Mandela*, Chrysalis/Two Tone CHS TT12 26 (1984), and *Bright Lights/Racist Friend*, Chrysalis/Two Tone CHS TT25 (1983).

127. Sade, *When Am I Going to Make a Living*, Epic TA 4437 (1984).

128. Fela Ransome Kuti, *Upside Down*, Decca WA, Aprodisic OW APS 2023 (1976), see John Darnton, "Nigeria's Dissident Superstar," *New York Times Magazine*, July 24, 1977, pp. 12, 22, 23.

129. Darnton, "Nigeria's Dissident Superstar," p. 23.

130. Fela Anikulapo Kuti and Africa 70, *Sorrow, Tears and Blood*, Kalakuta Records KK 001-A (1977), and *Unknown Soldier*, Phonodisk Skylark SKLP 003A (1979).

131. Fela Anikulapo Kuti and Africa 70, *Black President*, Arista Spart 1167 (1981), and *Original Sufferhead*, Arista Spart 1177 (1981).

132. Interview at Brixton Academy, London, December 12, 1983.

133. Jack Barron, "Africa and Bright," *Sounds*, July 7, 1983, p. 40.

134. Curtis May, "Loose in the Bush," *Black Music and Jazz Review*, April 1984, p. 17.

135. Jack Barron, "Takes a Shine to Hugh Masekela," *Sounds*, July 14, 1984, p. 34.

136. Juluka, *Scatterlings of Africa*, Safari Shake 1 (1982).

137. Mutabaruka, *Check It*, Alligator AL 8306 (1983).

138. Gil Scott-Heron, *From South Africa to South Carolina*, Arista Arty 121 (1976).

139. Danny Kelly, "Sound and Wordpower: Jimmy Cliff Talks About This, That and Everything," *New Musical Express*, September 8, 1984, p. 11.

140. Courtney Pine, *Journal to the Urge Within*, Island ILPS 9846 (1986).

3 *Revolution or Accommodation?*

The words that Frederick Douglass so eloquently penned in 1857 have not yet ceased to be appropriate for those who suffer discrimination or oppression:

If there is no struggle, there is no progress. Those who profess freedom and yet deprecate agitation are men who want crops without plowing. They want rain without thunder and lightning. They want the ocean without the awful roar of its mighty waters. Power concedes nothing without a demand. It never did and it never will.[1]

Songs sung by black people all over the world have echoed these sentiments. They have continuously contained exhortations to "struggle" against inequity and make "progress" toward freedom. But although the concepts of freedom and equality have remained constant as ultimate goals, they have always had variable connotations. Some people have aimed, and still aim, no higher than apparent freedom from racial discrimination. They accept the constraints imposed by their society on full equality and assume that if racial blocks are removed, they can make as much progress as any white person. Others, more percipiently, are aware that real racial equality can be achieved only alongside economic equality. They see racism as being an inherent characteristic of most capitalist systems, and think that these intrinsically exploitative forms of government need to be radically transformed before freedom from racial oppression can be assured. What they are all agreed on is the need for some form of change.

"Change" is a flexible word. Almost all black oppressed people have long sought change for their psychological and material betterment. To some this has meant a fight for equal opportunities, equal status, and equal regard or respect within whatever system operates. Adequate income and education, and equal legal and social rights, are seen as obvious prerequisites for a better life. Fundamental disagreement appears only as to the means. Many black and white thinkers believe it is unrealistic to expect an elitist capitalist system to relinquish its inbuilt need for an inferior, exploitable labor force that makes things easier if it can be identified by its color. Such critics of capitalism argue that only under a socialist system, where equality is as important as the needs of the individual, will such exploitation end. If the wealth of a country was shared equally rather than being owned by a small percentage of favored individuals (for instance, in Britain in 1984, 75 percent of the marketable wealth was owned by 25 percent of the people; in the United States, slightly more polarized figures were compounded by an acknowledged fall of 10 percent in workers' real income over the previous decade; in South Africa, 86 percent of the land is owned by the white 15 percent of the nation), there would be no need for discrimination on the basis of race or color.[2]

To achieve fundamental change, some kind of revolution will inevitably be necessary. Political theorists and songsters alike are divided as to whether this need involve violence and be more, rather than less, dramatic. The idea of "revolution" that is projected in song obviously can be immensely mutable, and as disparate as the systems to which people must otherwise accommodate. Yet the similarities are perhaps more constant then the differences. Almost all of the black singers whose lyrics are in English live in capitalist societies. Those who believe in accepting the system as a framework may be integrationist or black nationalist, but those who denounce that system are, with few exceptions, socialist. As Malcolm X so succinctly put it: "You can't have capitalism without racism. And if you find [antiracists] usually they're socialists or their political philosphy is socialism."[3]

Many would also accept and apply more widely the analysis applied by Huey Newton, leader of the Black Panthers, to the situation in the United States:

The blood, sweat, tears and suffering of black people are the foundation of the wealth and power of the United States of America. We were forced to build America, and if forced to, we will tear it down. The immediate result of this destruction will be suffering and bloodshed. But the end result will be perpetual peace for all mankind.[4]

Erika Huggins and Bobby Seale were both prominent members of the Black Panthers and obviously believe that popular art forms can be an important part of the struggle. In their introductions to *Shots*, a Liberation News Service book of photographs linked with appropriate revolutionary quotes, Seale sees such works as integral to the movement to overthrow oppression. Art that exposes the reality of exploitation can unite the exploited, "and we must move to smash the system, lest we fall victims to a destroyed earth." Once common problems are understood and faced—and street art and music can further that understanding—"we will realize that we are all-in-one part of the people's revolutionary struggle."[5] Dave Harker, a British socialist and writer of a book on politics and popular music, argues: "Although . . . music can't really topple the walls of Jericho, it may effect structural damage to bourgeois ideology, if the conditions are right."[6]

The attempt to "topple the walls of Jericho" began among black Americans in the earliest days of slavery. The spirituals were far more revolutionary than most people, until recently, have imagined. Close examination shows just how subversive they were, and it is not surprising that so many were used as "freedom songs" by the civil rights movement of the 1950s and 1960s. Songs like "Go Tell It on The Mountain," "We'll Never Turn Back," "Walk with Me, Lord," "Been in the Storm So Long," and "Freedom Train" were all spirituals being used a second time to stir up a spirit of resistance.

The original uses of the spirituals were manifold, but dominant was the determination to resist the oppression of slavery. Wherever possible, the power of the master over the daily lives of slaves would be subverted. The spirituals encouraged slaves to take as much control over their living and working conditions as possible, and spurred their determination to keep their spirits free from demeaning domination. They may have been 'buked and scorned," but they intended to

> Spread my wings and
> Fly, fly, fly.

There is also an unambivalent belief in freedom involving real justice and a full life:

> You got a right, I got a right
> We all got a right, to de tree of life.

And another spiritual claims, a right to live as well as the rich.

More extreme were the demands made by Louisiana slaves in some extraordinarily revolutionary songs. They sang not only of becoming free but also of guillotining or hanging their oppressive masters and overseers. Most of all, the spirituals positively encouraged and aided escape from slavery. Freedom from slavery is referred to in "Deep River":

> Deep river, my home is over Jordan,
> Deep river, Lawd, I wan' to cross
> over into camp ground.

Professor Lemuel Berry of Alabama State University School of Music points out that this

> . . ."is a song of defiance." . . . The phrase, "my home is over Jordan" actually represents the north (home) and the Ohio River (Jordan). Likewise, the phrase "that promised land where all is peace" refers to the freedom of the north. Deep River was an uplifting spiritual whch unlike its present status of being sung in a minor key (funerals) was often sung in a major key. Not only was the use of a major key significant, but, it raised the hope and aspiration of the slave[s] that one day they would be freed.[7]

"Go Down, Moses" has long been acknowledged as a key "runaway" song. With the help of Harriet Tubman, the slaves will escape the South and its slavery. It is also a stern warning to the South:

> Oppressed so hard they could
> Not stand
> Let my people go.

"My Lord, What a Morning" was consistently used to encourage escape through the Underground Railroad, the stars referred to in the song being a directional guide. "De Gospel Train" is even more explicit:

> De Gospel train's a comin'
> I hear it just at hand
> I hear de car wheels movin'
> An' rumblin' thro' the land
> De far is cheap, and all
> can go
> De rich an' poor are dere
> No second class aboard dis
> train
> No difference in de fare.

To Professor Berry this "shows an organized patter to rebel against slavery. The slaves are informed throughout this song that the abolitionists are near and they should prepare to leave." Berry goes on to point out that the slave is aware of all the problems created, and preconceived plans disturbed, by such escapes: "To rebel against the slave society is to rebel against the schematic structure of the southern economic trandition."[8] The owner lost money, manpower, and future productivity in a way that had no room for negotiation. "Steal Away" not only was used as a call to join the Underground Railroad and escape but also can be interpreted as an insurrectionist song.

Behind the basic desire for freedom was an implicit assumption that the northern states or Canada would provide not just escape from slavery but also untrammeled opportunities. Few wanted to return to the Africa of their forefathers. Most saw the nonslave states of America as the "promised land." Perhaps the allegiance of African-Americans could be expected to be thus since in almost 250 years no more than 400,000 slaves came to the United States from Africa. The vast majority of slaves in the southern states were American born, and to them this was not only the land of their birth but somewhere they could reach out for true liberty:

> I am bound for the promised land
> Who will come and go with me?[9]

References to thunder and lightning as agencies of change in apparent "escape" songs suggest a threat more fundamental than the odd slave quietly slipping away. When slaves participated in the organized rebellions that stopped short of being life threatening, the system was challenged but could be retrieved through negotiation. The master would retain his status and more of his power in return for better living and working conditions for the rebellious slaves. While all slaves resented the inequity of their position, some seemed to accept it as inevitable:

> The big bee flies high
> The little bee makes the honey
> The black folks make the cotton
> And the white folks get the money.[10]

Yet most made every attempt to make that system more equitable, to make it bend so that concessions to their humanity and their needs were made. Pressure from the slaves meant that on some plantations and farms, at various points in time and in various places, living conditions were better than they might have been. Through individual and collective efforts, slaves acquired the right to marry, occasionally to obtain an education, to buy and sell goods, and to purchase their own freedom. None of these rights was recognized by law, but they had a practical reality in certain times and places that made the law almost irrelevant. Almost but not quite—the threat of legal constraint always hung over slaves however many minor concessions they might win. Even when better working conditions and shorter hours were obtained, the ultimate goal of freedom was out of reach for all but the fortunate few, and better conditions were always dependent on the whim of the master.

There were also numerous slave songs that celebrated the ability of slaves to use their intelligence and wit to change a basically invidious system. The elemental lack of freedom was minimally compensated for by the freedom to trick the master and so win the freedom to dance the night away:

> Wear a red gown
> Feet de de diddle.

Slaves would even more eagerly dance to songs that showed the master as easy to overthrow rather than just outwit:

> Jackass rared
> Jackass pitched
> Throwed ol' massa in the ditch.

Paul Robeson was convinced that the spirituals were "the soul of the race made manifest," and he felt they should be cherished and used to illustrate the rich cultural heritage of black Americans.[11] Robeson was one of the most coherent and articulate black philosophers and activists of the early twentieth century. He believed that black Americans could participate in a new world culture as Africans and help the movement toward a "family of nations," an ideal he felt must be realized if the world was to survive. Robeson was not only a believer in the value of blackness but also an ardent socialist. He believed that only a movement toward socialism in America could produce real equality for black Americans. Instead of this movement, he witnessed a rise in antisocialist feeling that blocked black progress toward full participation in American democracy. He made himself a figure of censure when he denounced the United States for its imperialist, indeed fascist, policies toward Africa and praised the Soviet Union for treating Africans with respect and raising black people to full human dignity. His career as the greatest American interpreter of Shakespeare and as a formidable singer was in tatters because of his socialist convictions.

Almost as revolutionary was Robeson's insistence on performing concerts where the entire repertoire was composed of spirituals. He had become more certain, as he had studied African and European cultures in great depth, that the music of the slave belonged beside the greatest music produced anywhere.

Early in his political and philosophical explorations, Robeson became aware that equality and existing forms of capitalism seemed basically antipathetic. He came to believe that there was no reasonable doubt that socialism was a better and stronger way of life than any other, and sought to promote this ideal in song as much as in speech. For the rest of his life he insisted that only through socialism would the African heritage be maintained and encouraged, and the aspirations of black people be fulfilled.

Robeson also saw the blues, as well as the spirituals, as a rich embodiment of the black heritage and testament to black endurance and talent, but he felt less need to promote an already popular art form by frequent personal performances.

The blues were indeed a black American cultural form that provided an even more dense repository of both the African past and the current, day-to-day repsonses to personal and collective problems and situations. The bluesman or blueswoman was the accepted community spokesman (or spokeswoman) on social and political issues. Sometimes the views reflected were clear and straightforward, and amounted to a musical version of widely held views. Occasionally underlying fears and tensions, contradictions and confusions, were laid out in the music as the only way they could be expressed.

The aim of most black families was the essentially Jeffersonian ideal of becoming self-sufficient landowners. Bitterness crept into the blues songs that evolved during Reconstruction when it was realized that sharecropping was the nearest the average black family was to be allowed to get to land ownership. That bitterness increased when landlords refused to share the crops fairly and too many black families became more and more deeply enmeshed in unjust debts. Blues mourned the loss of a dream: the failure of the American system to allow the acquisition of land by any means and on almost any scale. Loans were refused, and attempts at joint ownership were frequently burned out by the Ku Klux Klan or kindred organizations. The few black-owned farms that did exist only made the dream more tantalizing.

At the close of the nineteenth century, Booker T. Washington assumed the role of the most accommodating black leader. The music similarly seemed to accept an unacceptable lot in life—for now, at least. But many songs had an undertone of resentment and menace that suggested the accommodation was more in overt behaviour than in basic feelings. It would not take long for those submerged feelings to struggle to the surface and reveal resentment and despair vying with the ethos of resignation. In Mississippi, Charley Patton sang a traditional "hard luck" blues:

> Hard luck is at your front door, blues are in your room
> Hard luck is at your front door, blues are in your room
> Callin' at your back door, what is gonna become of you.

Abandoning the South and its "accommodation" seemed the answer to many black families, and they migrated north in a search for real economic and political equality. They saw the North as a land of promise at a time when they were bemoaning the effect of the Mississippi bollweevil in song. More or less simultaneously, World War I created jobs in northern factories, and there was a massive migration to urban centers like Chicago, New York, Detroit, and Pittsburgh. Blues songs about traveling north were filled with anticipation. Some went over the top and depicted the streets of Chicago as paved with gold; others just talked of picking up bundles of dreams and hopping on a northbound train. In reality, migration led to the ghettoization of black people in northern cities. But despite riots and discrimination, hope that the system might provide more than a bare living did not die. It was hard to pay the unfairly high rents demanded of black families, but songs like Bessie Smith's *House Rent Blues* (Columbia 14032–D, 1924) and Lil Johnson's *House Rent Scuffle* (Vocalion 1410, 1929) were the cheerful blues of born survivors.

A strong survival instinct was more necessary then ever in the 1920s, a decade of extremes that saw the resurgence of the Ku Klux Klan. It was also a time when black power was matched with a desire for black people to achieve success as capitalists. There was a generalized campaign not to "buy where you can't work" and a more specific attempt by Marcus Garvey to establish black capitalist enterprises. Marcus Garvey was a Jamaican of enormous personal charisma who not only established the Universal Negro Improvement Association and popularized the phrase "black is beautiful" but also set up international trading companies such as the Black Star Line. Hazel Meyer's overly optimisitic *Black Star Line* (Pathe 032053, 1924) was released just as Garvey was arrested and imprisoned for mail fraud by promising profits the company could not deliver. The less successful aspects of capitalism lay exposed, but while hope lingered on, cynicism increased in the blues and in day-to-day attitudes.

Robert Johnson made one of the earliest and most disturbing critical evaluations of the very nature of the American dream in his 1930s blues. All the inherent contradictions of American ideals and aspirations are present in his music. The songs are so exploratory and inventive, so successful at reaching for and touching impossible chords and inexpressible emotions, that they seem to echo the promise and the possibilities held out by a society that claims everyone can rise to the top and be anything they want. At the same time and in the same songs, all the despair and desolation of knowing that the very things most desired are unattainable, blocked, and out of reach, echo in the inconsolable voice and unearthly guitar. The conflict between what America seems to offer and what it fails to deliver is all there in the eerie sounds and haunting words of songs like "Stones in My Passway" (*King of the Delta Blues Singers*, BS 62456):

> When you hear me howlin' in my passway, rider
> PLEASE open your door and let me in.

Greil Marcus, *Rolling Stone* writer and author of the brilliant *Mystery Train: Images of America in Rock 'n' Roll Music*, has said part of the power of Johnson's music lies in his "ability to shape the chaos and the lonelines of his betrayal or ours."[12]

Many of the other itinerant bluesmen from Mississippi, Texas, Louisiana, and the Carolinas complained about harsh conditions and injustice, but few advocated radical political change. Extreme personal or collective anwers were found, such as Roy Brown's promise to throw himself on his mother's tombstone and die, and Carl Martin's logical conclusion that if black deprivation continues, robbing and stealing would become inevitable. Any suggestion of a more fundamental revolution usually came in rather vague terms, such as Sleepy John Estes, "Everybody Ought to Make a Change" (*Down South Blues*, MCA 510–091, Jazz Heritage Vol. 48, 1935–1940).

The years of the Depression and the New Deal were times when black families suffered far more than white families from deprivation and unemployment. While the majority of blues songs expressed anger and disillusionment, there were some, like Blind Willie McTell's *Hillbilly Willie's Blues* (Decca 7117, 1935), that expressed only admiration for the president and the way he ran the country. More typical was Skip James's encapsulation of black deprivation in *Hard Time Killing Floor* (Paramount 13065): "Hard time nearly everywhere you go." To him times were "harder than ever been before."

There was still the stubborn belief that heaven on earth should be attainable, that the American dream should at least provide a good living. Since the New Deal failed to provide either jobs or a reasonable standard of relief for the vast majority of black people, most of their songs were along the more sarcastic lines of Carl Martin's "Let's Have a New Deal" (*Country Classics 4*). Even here, however, there was a flickering hope that sardonic prodding in song might lead to some improvement in living conditions.

The urban blues of Big Bill Broonzy, Sonny Boy Williams, Muddy Waters, and many more eloquent spokesmen also sang of troubles and deprivation, and blamed the government for failing to provide better welfare or living conditions. Few suggested that the structure of government should be changed. It is far more common for singers such as Bobo Jenkins to seek a solution in a change of parties. Jenkins had implicit faith in the Democrats' giving black people a better life (Bobo Jenkins, "Democrat Blues," *Country Blues Classics*, Vol. 12; *Blues Classics*).

Since the depressed 1930s Louis Jordan had played music that revolutionized sound—he certainly helped create R&B, and his saxophone provided the dominant new musical element. He was not, however, an obvious political revolutionary. His lyrics seemed to urge people to push for acceptance within the existing scheme of things. His "Open the Door, Richard" and "Keep a Knockin'" used humor and innuendo to attack discrimination.[13]

Just as Louis Jordan has been described as a bluesman, an early progenitor of R&B, and a superb jazzman, Billie Holiday also crossed musical boundaries and refused to fit neatly into any category. However she is defined, she was an immensely powerful and popular singer, and she wrote one extraordinarily influential song about her perspective on discrimination. Billy Holiday's "God Bless the Child" (*Billie Holiday*, Vol. II, MCA MCA1776) is not just a song that became a black anthem, it is very obviously a song that highlights lack of faith in the American system. In it Billie Holiday recognizes that the way society functions means that those who already "have" enough are the ones who will "get" more. Her answer is for black people, individually and collectively, to be self-reliant. In her own case, she had no choice. The world's greatest jazz singer always had to fend for herself. In a hostile world, she survived by relying on her own resources. Neither the system around her nor her family, friends, or lovers did much to help—more often they were negative forces. That she died young was not surprising; that she took so much on for so long was a triumph.

This survival impulse was a characteristic black people had nurtured during slavery and had found to be invaluable in the years since then, while equality was being pursued like an elusive butterfly. The harmonica ace, Elder Wilson, recorded several songs in Detroit during the 1940s that show a determination to seek real change. In songs that link up with the slave past and reach out to the future, he urges people "Better Get Ready" to get on "This Train" and be prepared for some substantial changes. He had certainly had enough of an existence full of "Troubles Everywhere."[14] In a similar way the magnificent John Lee Hooker sang "Trouble Blues," "The Road Is

Rough," and "Want Ad Blues" with acerbic, critical lyrics and fero-
cious guitar solos on *Everbody Rockin'* (Charly R and B CRB 1014)
in the 1950s. Before the 1960 election, in "Democrat Man" John Lee
Hooker (*Blue*! Fontana FJL 119, 1960) was determined to vote
Democrat in the next election, and believed that the Democrats
would solve all the problems of poverty and welfare. A few years
later he was among those virulently criticizing the government over
Vietnam, and his cynicism seemed to spill over into a general dis-
belief that internal exploitation or deprivation would be dealt with in
a reasonable or effective way by the government.

In "Life Is a Nightmare," Juke Boy Bonner sees life as a "nightmare" full of "shattered dreams" in which "people are trying to keep
you down." This son of a Texas sharecropper saw music not only as a
way out of poverty but also as a means of articulating his anger and
frustration and those of people in similar circumstances. In "It's Time
to make a Change," he advises people not to put up with any more
suffering either in relationships or in life in general. In "Stay off Lions
Avenue" he meets a situation too dire to change, where people have
sunk to such depths that they will kill while being unaware of what
they are doing. The only way out is to fight for a better system, he
advises in "Struggle Here in Houston."[15]

Yet moderation and hope are the keynote of a very large number
of blues and R&B singers. Possibly the most representative view is
that of Eddie Clearwater. He wants to believe in the American dream
and extols the virtues as well as the difficulties of coming "up the hard
way." Doubts creep more fully into his songs as he dwells on the fact
that "the world is in a bad situation"—and he means his world, the
American world.[16] He seems reluctant to do anything that will substantially change that world. Others were less circumspect, and R&B
was often the medium used to express subversive attitudes that were
based on a belief that the system itself could accommodate change.

R&B in the 1950s had become the music of teenage rebellion. It
was relabeled "rock and roll," and the new term was sometimes
justified by the country element that was occasionally added to the
basic R&B format. It was also a music that was quintessentially
integrated. Its roots were undeniably black, but its most successful
practitioners were both black and white. Chuck Berry, Bo Diddley,
Fats Domino, and Little Richard shared *Billboard* pop chart success
with Elvis Presley, Jerry Lee Lewis, Buddy Holly, and Bill Haley. All
too often white "copies" of black songs sold more records than the

black originals, but black singers were speaking to and for white as well as black youth.

Chuck Berry's songs, for instance, were symbols of rebellious youth in the affluent America of the 1950s. He could be critical, as he was in "School Days" and "Back in the U.S.A.," but he believed that, like the teenagers he related to so well, he could make it in the American system. He was acknowledged at the time as the supreme architect of rock and roll, and his lyrical mastery was regarded as highly as his consummate and original skill as a guitarist and showman. Only slowly did Berry become embittered as he realized that he would never gain the wealth or the acceptance that came so easily to his white counterparts. Gradually rock and roll became a sound that was associated predominantly with white performers. It became obvious that it was not the liberating force it had once seemed.

The liberation role was transferred to soul music, and a number of black artists managed to top the sales charts in both soul and rock and roll categories. There were some singers, such as Sam Cooke, with such enormous range and talent that straddling apparently separate genres seemed effortlessly simple. Sam Cooke's 1965 smash hit "A Change Is Gonna Come" (*The Man and His Music*, RCA PL87127(2)) predicted the "immenent" arrival of a major change. The nature of the transformation was unspecified. The only clue was that an appeal to a "brother" not only went unanswered but resulted in bringing him to his knees. This hardly showed an optimistic faith in the existing system, but it certainly fell short of actually advocating revolutionary change. The swelling, melismatic voice with its rounded confidence expressed more positive hope than the words themselves: that this long awaited "change" would really improve people's lives in some tangible way.

For much of the 1950s and 1960s the civil rights struggle for integration epitomized the height of many black aspirations. In the South especially, people marched or "sat in" at lunch counters to win equal access to transportation, social facilities, and education. Many civil rights marchers' songs emphasized the desirability of integrating into the system. Traditional spirituals were adapted to be more applicable to the times:

> I'm so glad segregation got to go
> I'm so glad segregation got to go
> I'm so glad segregation got to go
> Singing glory hallelujah
> I'm so glad

I'm so glad intergration on its way
I'm so glad intergration on its way
I'm so glad intergration on its way
Singing glory hallelujah
I'm so glad.

While such songs were used by activists, Aretha Franklin's version of "Respect" (*Aretha's Greatest Hits*, Atlantic 240018 Super, 1970) became a symbol for all black people in the 1960s. It marked the continuing hope that segregation would disappear, and that black Americans could be treated as full and equal citizens and get all the "respect" that was their due. The song seemed to embody the expectations that the integrationist policies supported by the Supreme Court's decision in *Brown* v. *Board of Education of Topeka* in 1954 and the integration of the buses in Montgomery, Alabama, in 1955–1956 had sparked off. Martin Luther King, Jr., had emerged as the leader of the civil rights movement as a result of the Montgomery bus boycott. He had organized marches throughout the South to bring integration closer, and he had helped students begin their onslaught on lunch counters and voter registration with the founding of The Student Non-Violent Coordinating Committee. (SNCC).

When Martin Luther King was shot in April 1968, every major city across the United States exploded into flames. If the greatest advocate of nonviolence the Western world has known ended up shot, what hope was there for advancement without force? Some were aware that King had become dangerous as he had moved closer to a socialist ideal when he carried banners such as "Power for Poor People." Black Americans mourned and rioted because they venerated him for a variety of reasons. As part of the riot control policies, James Brown came on nationwide TV and told the rioters to get back in their homes like good law-abiding citizens. His behaviour may have seemed out of character since James Brown's music had an intrinsic excitement and sense of danger that could be interpreted as menacing. But, in reality, he posed no threat to the established mores of society. Some of his greatest hits—"Sex Machine" and "It's a Man's, Man's, Man's World"—were hymns to male supremacy, and any of his other successes that dealt with the sociopolitical system were supportive of the American dream. James Brown himself had "made it" from Georgia poverty to immense wealth, and saw himself as a realization of the opportunities offered by this land of his birth. Only recently has his antinuclear, antiwar series of records with such symbolic subversives as Afrikaa Bambaataa and Johnny Lydon begun to shake his conservative image.

Despite all this, it cannot be denied that James Brown's anthemic song "Say It Loud—I'm Black and I'm Proud" (King 6187, 1968) had a rousing impact on America. Black pride and black achievement were already issues raised by Malcolm X, the Black Panthers, and SNCC—among many—but here was a disk of undeniable assertiveness that blasted out from millions of radios as a challenge and an encouragement. It did, after all, leave open the question of just how black pride was to become real and how equality was to be achieved. It was a song that could be used by black nationalists, or black socialists, or anyone black as an assertion of the worth of their blackness. The dangerous element, the challenge in the song, came with the pounding urgency of the bass and drums, and the stridently demanding horns. It also was there in the words that refused to stop agitation until "we get what we deserve." Less exciting, but more characteristic, were the words of "Don't Be a Dropout" (King 6056, 1966), telling black people to support the system, to work toward full acceptance and equality within it.

Many other soul singers took King's ideals and words extremely seriously, and used them as a foundation for some politically dynamic songs. Solomon Burke's *I Have a Dream* (ABC DSX–50161, 1974) begins with a quote from King asserting that *his* dream was deeply rooted in the American dream. Burke refers to walking hand in hand and the attainment of a "better land." He sings of "love and peace." He also sings of "freedom and liberty." It could be significant that his last words on that track are—"the impossible dream!" In "Now Is the Time," on the same album—he sings, "We must believe in the land we live in with a little more faith." In "Social Change," the change Burke foresees is in himself and his newfound ability to get to the top. He's determined to be a winner within the system. Billy Paul took Paul McCartney's song "Let 'Em In" (*Greatest Hits*, CBS RIR 32347, 1980) and gave the lyrics a fresh urgency with the addition of extracts from Martin Luther King, Jr., and Malcolm X. King's "I Have a Dream" speech featured prominently and dictated the mood of the entire number. Stevie Wonder's "Happy Birthday" (*Hotter Than July*, Motown 2C070–64121, 1980) was not only homage to the philosophy and political leadership of Martin Luther King, Jr.; it was also part of a campaign to make the nonviolent activist's birthday a national holiday. The song itself included extracts from King's speeches. It continued the trend started by Solomon Burke and projected King as less radical than he actually was. "Someday" by The Gap Band (*Total Experience 5*, 1983) also used extracts from Martin Luther King, Jr.—and for good measure Stevie Wonder popped up on the single as well. Bobby Womack's *Poet* and *Poet II* (Motown 2L72705, 1984) also sought black advancement without undermining the existing structure of society. "American Dream" is yet another number with extracts from King's "I Have a Dream" speech, and echoes his early optimism about the possible realization of that dream through peaceful means.

Not unexpectedly, Michael Jackson is highly supportive of the American system. In "Beat It" (EPIC EPCA3258) he urges ghetto kids to "beat" all their disadvantages and the bad influence of the street, and make it in the system. The sales of *Thriller* alone have made Jackson a multimillionaire, and for him the system self-evidently has worked. His closeted life makes him unaware of just how badly the American dream not only has failed to benefit the majority of black Americans, but also has deliberately kept most of them at the bottom of the economic pyramid that makes the very existence of that dream possible. Equally unrealistic and remarkably similar in sentiment, is Donna Summer's disco-rock number "Living in America," which would have the listener believe in a fairy tale of gas pump attendant one day, Hollywood superstar the next.

More realistic lyrically and more innovative musically was a number by Earth, Wind and Fire. They fused jazz, soul, and funk in a fresh way, but they were hardly a politically dangerous band. Nevertheless, according to the *New Musical Express*, "Freedom of Choice," on the album *Powerlight*, was banned from U.S. national radio because it advocated that black people should exercise their right to vote.[17] Being right in the politically unmenacing mainstream was evidently still hazardous in the mid-1980s. A similar situation existed in the actual political situation in the South a few years earlier. Growing strength in the late 1960s made the Southern Conference Educational Fund a force to be reckoned with. It was an interracial organization that fought poverty and injustice, and set up a project in the deep South called Grass Roots Organizing Work (GROW). It began to build a political coalition between black and white workers, and ran candidates for local elections as the Workers'

Independent Party. Its aims were to establish a government control-led by poor and working people and to introduce real equality. Activists in this movement, such as Walter Collins and Joe Malloy, found themselves hounded by the government and forced out of action. Farm workers' cooperatives were similarly discouraged and found their land, literally, disappearing from under their feet.

Astutely steering clear of any direct political references, Larry Blackmon of Cameo says that his band is "in the business of per-petuating success." He and the band are totally in control of them-selves as a "product," from the making of the music and videos to packaging their image: "We like to think of ourselves as showing how free freedom of expression can be. Cameo is saying that 'we're gonna do just what the hell we want to do.'"[18] Blackman's obvious intel-ligence would prevent him from imagining that every black American could enjoy the same freedom and success, but he is prepared to settle for parodying that dream and establishing success for himself, his band, and those linked with it as at least a start. He also reaffirms the supremacy of black music as the most innovative cultural force in America.

Bobby McFerrin believes that music is not a tool for success but a force for good in the world. He optimistically sings of a "Jubilee" (*Bobby McFerrin*, Elektra Musician MUSK 52387, 1982) where "everyone is free" and "happiness abounds," and there's even "danc-ing on the sea." Using his voice as a spontaneous and immensely flexible instrument, he interacts fluidly with Victor Feldman's piano, Rhodes Larry Klein's bass, and John Guerin's evocative drums. Just how this state of nirvana is to be reached is left to the individual listener to decide, but the music is clearly intended as an aid to getting there.

Harold Melvin and The Blue Notes sound far more materialistic when they sing "Reaching for the World." They want success—material success—and condemn those who are just looking for a good time. What they want, however, does require fundamental change if more than a limited few are to overcome immense obstacles simply "to survive."[19]

Not surprisingly, Kool and The Gang are all in favor of accom-modation. They want to win in the existing system. They echo Curtis Mayfield's call for people to "get ready," but here it's a summons to get to the top and take places at the top of the system. *Victory* (written by Khalis Bayyon and James Taylor), a hit single in 1987 for the band, supports the perpetual illusion that sustains the American dream when it claims that everyone can win.

Curtis Mayfield is unique in his genius but representative of the views of the black community in his attempt to promote both reform of and acceptance within the system. The possibility of more radical change is there in his songs, but it is a last resort. If people can "move on up" without a revolution of any dramatic dimensions, he is perfectly happy to accept that. But he is always clear that he wants everyone to be "a winner," to "keep on pushin'" so that he can genuinely sing "we're moving on up" on *We're a Winner*.[20] Curtis Mayfield and The Impressions had always sung about creating better conditions and a better life for black people. "Keep on Keeping On" (*Roots*, Buddah Super 2318–045) and "Move On Up" were exhortations not to give up on the fight for equality. Yet criticism of the actual system is only implied, never spelled out, and all The Impressions' songs can be interpreted as supporting black efforts to win equality within the framework of American capitalism. "People Get Ready," despite its religious overtones, has more of an air of menace and danger about it. It somehow seems to be more fundamentally subversive. In "Beautiful Brother of Mine" (*Roots*), Mayfield has no doubt that time spent on self-education and consciousness raising in the ghettos has resulted in a unity of aim and determination that will push all opposition out and successfully lead to the attainment of freedom and equality.

Underneath all this, Curtis Mayfield seems to be a natural subversive. He is certainly no doctrinaire revolutionary but he instinctively recognizes basic injustice and has systematically denounced the discrimination inherent in American capitalism. In "Underground" (*Roots*) he imagines a totally new society developing under the ashes, rather than rising from them, of the self-destruction that seems the present destination. He predicts or hopes that there will be equality in the "underground" and that judgments of fellow men will cease: "We'll all turn black. . . . Color, creed, and breed must go."

These sentiments would have been approved by the most revolutionary voice in America: that of Malcolm X in the months preceding his assassination. In 1964 and 1965 he abandoned black nationalism and the Black Muslims in favor of a sophisticated form of international socialism. His political philosophy provided the inspiration for black socialist movements over the next few decades.

In the late 1960s and early 1970s the Black Panthers, led by Huey Newton and Bobby Seale, sought a real revolution. They wanted a black and white working-class alliance that would place power in the hands of the people and remove it from the corrupt and decadent government that exploited the black and the poor. They were realistic enough to be aware that such a revolution could be a long time coming and that change was essential in the immediate future. Bobby Seale and Elaine Brown, deputy minister of information for the Panthers, were candidates in the local election in Oakland, California, and Elaine Brown was elected to the city council.

Like many other black activists and singers, Brown sang on her album *Seize the Time* (Vault 131 1971) of seizing the time for real revolution as well as making the most positive advances possible within the existing system. Not suprisingly, she went on to become the leader of the party once Newton was forced into exile. In her title song she chastises the passive and falsely agitatory who have "never even fought" for liberty or thought "to seize the time." In the "End of Silence" she argues that the time to be silent has passed and now the battle must be fought with guns. In the latter song the music is slow and darkly brooding, whereas in the first the sound is a clarion call to arms, and intensity is whipped up with the speed and tension of Elaine Brown's powerful vocals. Yet in some of the songs, such as "Poppa's Come Home," she concentrates on the need to build up the strengths of the black family—a traditional view that can still be seen as an appropriate element in the revolutionary process.

Huey Newton explained that the most radical revolutionary socialist demands were not anti-American; they were simply

an extension of the American Revolution of 1776. . . . This was truly a revolutionary struggle. Unfortunately, Blacks, because of racism in the country and the fact of slavery were not included in these rights. So, after this, we had the Civil Rights Movement, in order to gain those rights that whites gained in 1776. Some two hundred years have passed and we haven't gained those basic rights.

Of course, the country was not revolutionized even though there was a revolutionary movement. It was not revolutionized simply because production wasn't at the stage where a socialist development was encouraged by the other forces. . . . Blacks are still struggling for basic human rights; the right to vote, the right for economic well-being, etc. We cannot gain our political liberties without the economic freedom . . . our one goal is to crush American Capitalism and American Imperialism. Because without this, we can do nothing.[21]

These views were far more popular than has generally been assumed. A *Wall Street Journal* sampling of black opinion in January 1970 in four cities (San Francisco, New York, Cleveland, and Chicago) showed a clear majority of black people supported the aims and methods of the Panthers.

Other cities demonstrated their support for socialist ideals. In the late 1960s in Detroit, a black newspaper called *Inner City Voice* was selling 10,000 copies per week. This was no mean achievement, since it was run by John Watson as the mouthpiece of a group of dedicated Marxist-Leninist revolutionary socialists. Their clear-cut aim was the destruction of capitalism, and they attacked black nationalism as likely to lead only to a change of masters—black capitalists exploiting black workers. Watson reminded his readers that Huey Newton had said from jail that all black people ought to be socialists.

In the late 1960s and early 1970s music became a conscious tool in this movement toward a revolution. The most obvious functional was the album cut by Elaine Brown. On the inner sleeve she denounces capitalism as exploitative and explains that the Black Panthers want to create conditions where people "can begin to cooperate with each other" and end the illusion that it is necessary to take from others in order to survive. She calls on all working-class and unemployed people of every color to take the power that belongs to them. She hopes that her songs can help people shake off delusions implanted by the ruling elite so that they can reclaim the right to control their own destinies.

Archie Shepp's "Poem for Malcolm," recorded in 1969, was a cry of pain for the death of the most radical and influential of all black Americans. Accompanied by drums, bass, and piano, he sang of the need for "revolution," and he shouted out the word "revolution" with such vehemence that he seemed to be providing the inspiration and the will for a whole generation.[22]

In the late 1960s, Sly Stone's music acquired an overtly radical tone. It had always been revolutionary in nature. It fused soul, blues, jazz, psychedelic rock, and funk in a new way, and his bassist, Larry Graham, created the funk bass slap. Lyrically, however, the music slowly became more radical. *Stand!*, a powerful single and album, made an assertive appeal for racial understanding. There was an implied threat, but nothing overt or specific. The follow-up album, *There's a Riot Goin' On*, was far more dangerous. The title track was absent, but the whole album was permeated by a dark and brooding sense of menace. Greil Marcus sees *Riot* as "an exploration of and pronouncement on the state of the nation . . . black music, black politics, and a white world." The most disturbing track was undoubtedly "Thank You for Talkin' to Me, Africa." To Marcus, "There is no vocal music in rock 'n' roll to match it." The heavy bass line emphasizes the holocaustic anger in the words and voice that describe a battle with a gun-toting "devil" where bullets chase and maim until victory is won.[23] All the disappointment over the failed hopes of the 1960s and all the frustrated aggression were channeled into this dark song that warned of the necessity of meeting violence with violence and the need to take what society in its present form refused to give.

The early 1970s saw records rising high in the charts that "represented the most politicized black music in the history of rock 'n' roll."[24] This was living proof that people would buy records with politically disturbing and disruptive lyrics. They succumbed to numbers like Jerry Butler's tough, disillusioned "Only the Strong Survive" (*The Best of Jerry Butler*, Mercury 61281), which reached no. 4 in the *Billboard* charts, and the Chilites' "(For God's Sake) Give More Power to the People" (*Chilites Greatest Hits*, Brunswick 954185), which got to no. 26.

Some records, like Marvin Gaye's *What's Goin' On* album, were concept albums that also contained successful singles. Marvin Gaye was the most troubled of these articulate remonstrators. He never mentioned revolution, but he questioned every aspect of the American dream and indicated its self-evident failure in his probing lyrics. It was as if he had lived in a dream for years, then had suddenly been struck by the lightning of reality. This sudden jolt of illumination showed up the "dream" as a shabby farce that promised success but, in the tradition of the best "con" artists, almost always failed to deliver. No one listening, really listening, could fail to be at least discomforted and, more likely, acutely disillusioned. This was a single and an album that made people question every unproven political assumption that confronted them. Eyes that had only seen "through a glass darkly" now acquired new clarity of vision, and the fresh lens was ground with a more critical focus.

The Temptations also sent shock waves through an attentive nation. They changed from singing bland, comfortable songs to pouring out numbers charged with menace and creative tension. The percussion now danced around the drum, and the guitars were wilder than in most soul records. Against this compelling background the

Temptations poured out warnings that the unequal, inhuman state of affairs could not continue. In "Message from a Black Man," "Ball of Confusion," and "Unite the World" a change for the better was demanded rather than just desired. "Message from a Black Man" was one of the Temptations' most impassioned demands for change. "Moreover . . . because I'm coming through," they sang. "No matter how hard you try, you can't stop me now." The song also questioned the pairing of white and right—"together we stand, divided we fall." The falsetto sung by Eddie Kendricks soars over Dennis Edwards's rich, assertive bass, and the criss crossing, snare-driven rhythms were made for compulsive listening. The congas underlined the intensity while synthesizers swirled sound around with an insistence that almost matched the depth of Dennis Edwards's vocals. In "Ball of Confusion (That's What the World Is Today)," the Temptations reject the world as it is and mock the promises of politicians who say "Vote for me, and I'll set you free."[25] Even when the decade flipped into the 1980s, the Temptations were still recording radical songs like "Power," which the group described as "highly political. We got caught up in the riots of Miami and the jocks were saying '*oh, no, five black guys talking about taking the masses and moving mountains.*' They didn't trust it."[26]

There was another musician developing his talent at this moment in time whose mistrust of established societal, economic, and political mores and conventions was as near complete as possible. He expressed this rejection by breaking every musical convention. Jimi Hendrix produced some of the most powerful and rebellious sounds ever heard in black or white music. His guitar blasted out notes like bullets from a gun, and they targeted people's comfortable expectations and pretensions. Hendrix made music that was new and disturbing. His guitar wailed and shouted with a resonant eloquence no one had ever heard before. His brilliant experimental solos questioned everything about the music and the society that had produced it. Some numbers, like "Machine Gun," carried through the attack with aggressive lyrics. Most of all, he redefined what the guitar as an instrument was capable of, and by extending its limits, he seemed at the same time to open up psychological and political possibilities.

Among the really popular black American groups there is little doubt that the Isley Brothers are responsible for some of the more radical music. At the start of their career they often sang other people's "good time" songs with gospel-type effects on labels such as

RCA, Wand (a subsidiary of Scepter), and Motown. A considerable number of R&B and pop chart successes enabled them to start their own record company, T-Neck, and write and produce their own songs. One of their biggest hits that they also wrote was the assertive "Fight the Power" (*Forever Gold*, T-Neck 34452, 1975), where the thundering guitar echoes the frequently repeated directive to "fight the powers that be." "Harvest for the World," recorded the following year, but on the same album, asked for a more equitable sharing of the world's resources—an end to the situation where half the people are satisfied and half are in dire need.

On the 1977 album *Go for Your Guns* (Epic EPC 86027), Ernie Isley's flamboyant guitar shows a debt to Hendrix, while Chris Jasper entices fresh sounds out of his synthesizer. Here the accommodation of "Climbing up the Ladder" and "believin' in a dream" is offset by the tough "Go for Your Guns." A few years later "Caravan of Love" sought very basic changes in the American system.

There is no ambivalence about Nina Simone's "Revolution," which owes little to the Beatles and everything to centuries of frustration. The discordant, clashing, loud instrumentation spells imminent danger, and Nina's dramatic delivery leaves no doubt that the idea of a revolution is serious. She is impassioned in her belief that the American Constitution is "gonna have to bend" or be destroyed.[27]

On the album *Survival* (Philadelphia International Records PIR 80765, 1976) The O'Jays make equally clear demands in "Give the People What They Want"—for "equality, freedom" and "justice." They feel it is reasonable also to demand enough food to eat and a good education. They will go for whatever is necessary to provide that. In "The Rich Get Richer," The O'Jays attack the inequalities of the American system with tough lyrics and a hard beat. They mention that 16 families control the wealth of the world; they always win— "how in the world can they lose?" At the same time "people are starving and babies are crying." There's got to be a better way, they claim, a way that will end such obscene inequality. A year later they were even more forcible in putting over the message that people should "stand up" for "freedom" and "rights."[28]

Wilton Felder's song "Inherit the Wind" (*Inherit the Wind*, MCA MCG4013, 1979) talks of the "wind" bringing people to a "better day." More significantly, he also sings of the "storm" that grows inside people and a "sure" destiny. The symbolism acquires even more idealized aspirations when toneless rainbows are involved alongside the increasing strength of the propelling wind. It does not take an imaginative leap to think that Felder is advocating a far more ideal form of society in which people can realize their full potential and really inherit the wind.

Stevie Wonder also seeks a transformed society without "segregation" or "exploitation" in "Pastime Paradise," and in his classic "Livin' for the City" he darkly prophesies that if things don't change, the world may soon be over.[29] 24 Carat Black, a cult band in the black areas of American cities in the early 1970s went further and pushed for revolutionary action on *Ghetto: Misfortunes Wealth* (Stax Enterprises, ENS 1030, 1973).

August Darnell/Kid Creole argues that it is the people with chart success who have an obligation to speak out for change. They have the power to change minds. "Success for me," he says, "will be a tool for me to open my mouth louder and larger and a lot of 'truths' and 'realities' will be shattered." He smashes the idea that the American dream works. He has friends in the Bronx with enough talent and determination to get out and succeed: "today they're pumping gas: to me that proves they couldn't get out of the Bronx. God knows they tried. These were dreams shattered." He goes on to say that he could "speak out . . . through the music," guided by "his sharp social awareness, and an intensive conviction that wrongs are made to be righted."[30]

Many singers reflect the more extreme aspirations of Black Panthers like Erika Huggins, who in the early 1970s wanted power taken into the hands of the people and the decadent, existing political and social structures actually overthrown. Sweet Honey in the Rock is an all-woman a cappella band that refuses to compromise or accommodate. Their extensive repertoire, which they write, is rich in songs like "Ella's Song" (*Listen to the Rhythm*, SPIN106, 1983)—"We who believe in freedom cannot rest until it comes"—and focus their efforts on "teaching others to stand up and fight."

In a familiar way Gil Scott-Heron uses music to promote the idea of change as serious revolution. "The Revolution Will Not Be Televised," and music must be used to change the world. In "Black History of the World" (*Moving Target*, Arista AL906, 1983), to the background of Ron Holloway's ever eloquent sax, he sings of the world changing its rhythms "to the throbbing of unrest" as the "music reaches everyone." Through music, he believes, "we can change the world." Scott-Heron's lack of faith in the American political system's providing equality for black people is emphasized in "(You Can't Depend on) the Train from Washington" (*Real Eyes*, Arista AL9540, 1980). Politicians can be depended on only for "a bad position," and their "sleight of mouth will dazzle you." In "Washington D.C." Scott-Heron pinpoints the irony of this symbolic capital of democracy's being filled with "citizens of poverty."

When interviewed in June 1985 by this author, Scott-Heron was anxious to do anything possible to improve employment opportunities and protect the basic right to an adequate level of welfare. He pointed out:

There are more white folks on welfare than there are black people, but the manner in which Reagan tries to express it gives one the indication that only black folks are on welfare, so if he cuts it, only black people would be hurt, and therefore a lot of the right-wing folks that are out there where he is go along with it. But I think that when the farmers come to protest, when the steelworkers come to protest, when the coal miners come to protest, when the teachers come to protest, when the doctors come to protest, when the students come to protest, then you are saying that it's not just any one particular section that might be punished by the things he is trying to do. What we are trying to do is show that these are a broad base of people who are being offended and affected by the things he does, and try and influence them to be more vocal about the things they feel they need to be done. You see, ignoring something does not cure it. We are trying to help people to be more vocal in their objections to what's happening—every citizen has a voice, has a potential, and we are trying to encourage people to use it.[31]

Although Scott-Heron was born in Chicago and grew up in an equally blues-steeped area of Tennessee, he moved to New York and got a reputation as a superb exponent of the art of rap. Other early rap artists, such as the Last Poets, have similarly strong ideas about freedom and equality.

Rap in the very early 1970s was the most revolutionary of music. Before this New York DJing syndrome hit the streets at the end of the decade, backed by the electro funk initiated by Kraftwerk and refined by experts like Arthur Baker, Afrikaa Bambaataa, and The Sugarhill Rappers, The Watts Prophets were best sellers in every black ghetto. In 1971 they produced *Rappin' Black in a White World* (ALA, 1971). In it they unambivalently demanded a real "revolution." They referred to the riots that had inflamed cities in the 1960s and said, "them niggers ain't playing—and we won't either." On the contrary, they were deadly serious. Listing the endless crimes of

America against humanity and black people, they mourned black martyrs and girded themselves with words for the coming decisive battle when real freedom would be fought for unstintingly. Voices are the main instrumentation—and they are used as finely honed instruments in discordant harmony. Occasionally a cello provides stark counterpoint to the impatient, angry voices. This music is unambivalently a call to action.

The Last Poets also always wanted more than "bullshit changes." On *Oh My People* (Celluloid, CAL208, 1985) they denounce Reagan in "Hold Fast" and advocate revolution in "Get Movin.'" They had been making similar demands for a revolutionary popular uprising as early as the late 1960s and early 1970s. Their anger has remained constant—only their chauvinism in frequently resung numbers like "The Pill" prevents them from being the most fully radical of groups.

Once New York rap hit the airwaves and shot up the pop charts, more people became aware of the discontent stored in this traditional street art. Kurtis Blow missed early chart success, but Grandmaster Flash and the Furious Five pounded upward and onward with "*The Message*" (Sugarhill SHL 117, 1982). Hailed by many critics as the most radical record of the year, it actually stopped short of advocating any form of revolution. What it did was enunciate very clearly exactly what was wrong with life for a black man in America.

One of the toughest rap records was by Brother D on the Clappers label. In "How We Gonna Make the Black Nation Rise," Daryl Aamaa Nubyahn, a young Bronx math teacher, described the horrors of the Ku Klux Klan and the likelihood that its violence would get worse if black people didn't unite and fight. In a similar way Run DMC proved unambivalently that hip hop can be a medium not just for the release of energy through movement and the use of Hendrix-style, heavy guitar but also for the transmission of subversive and revolutionary political ideas. Their ideas were certainly more challenging than the simple support of Jesse Jackson as presidential candidate on Melle Mel's *Jesse* and Face 2000's *Run, Jesse, Run*.

Afrikaa Bambaataa, one of the most interesting and diversified rap artists, attempts to use the music as a force for action. He has established youth clubs in New York to divert energy from street violence with constructive creativity. He sees violence as endemic in American society and hopes that the energy it involves can be redirected toward positive change. He also warns that the "only time America really listens is when somebody starts getting violent back."

Bambaataa is a disciple of Malcolm X, and has used speeches by him, by other ministers of the Nation of Islam, and by Martin Luther King, Jr. on the inspirational *Trans-Europe Express*.[32]

Arguably the ultimate rap record is that made by the ultimate revolutionary socialist, Malcolm X (*No Sell Out*, Tommy Boy TB840B, 1983). Keith Le Blanc "cut up" some of Malcolm X's magnificently charismatic and convincing speeches, and came up with an electro-funk backing track that emphasized the words that centered on understanding the "truth" of the situation and dealing with that truth rather than selling out. The sounds of gunfire match the words warning of dramatic upheaval, but there are no confining orders. The listener is left to work out the best way to achieve a real revolution in present times. Yet how effective can any music be in catalyzing action? In an article on black protest music, Edna Edet said in 1976: "The black man has sublimated his grief in song for over 340 years and to many, this time for singing is past. The time for waiting is past."[33] Nona Hendrix carries this idea further on a number she calls "Revolutionary Dance" when she knows that the time for submission is gone and freedom—real, not just sung for—tangible freedom—must prevail.[34]

But to Amiri Baraka, any of the words he writes, speaks, or raps to music are essentially a specific call to action and are not simply ideas to be absorbed. In 1981 he set radical words to experimental jazz played by David Murray and Steve McCall. Over Murray's sensitive saxophone and McCall's adventurous percussion, Baraka talked of "Class Struggle in Music." He exulted in the strength of black culture, especially the brilliant, truthful music, and argued that this tradition was telling people plainly to "fight" for freedom from the chains of exploitation.[35] For Baraka the division between poetry and song has no real meaning, since he believes in the strength of black folk culture and the black oral tradition in which poetry is musical and lyrics are poetic. In this performance the words and music enhance and extend, each giving deeper resonance and meaning to every word and syllable, and making it very clear that black Americans are prepared to fight for real change. The live performance and the recording are certainly intense and dynamic enough to convince the apathetic that forceful action is essential if equality is to be gained.

The irony of the choices made by both singers and political activists is that the leap into the unknown territory of revolutionary socialism is actually the safest choice. To go on believing that the American system will ever provide equality is more than blindly optimistic. The evidence of 400 years of economic exploitation and social and political discrimination is weighted against any vain hope that American capitalism will ever provide anything more than an illusory American dream. This is a system that for too long has relied too heavily on massive unemployment, underemployment, and the underpaying of the lower levels of the work force to suddenly become transformed into the egalitarian paradise aimed for in the Declaration of Independence. Capitalist systems elsewhere are usually based on the American or European models, and can provide only mirages. A socialist system that is based on the devolution of power into the hands of the people themselves may be relatively untried, but it offers far more real expectation that every person can reach his or her full potential and share in the resources and wealth of a country.

The situation in Jamaica is far more confusing than in the United States. Socialism has never been more than a dream in North America, whereas in Jamaica both Michael Manley and Edward Seaga have organized governments masquerading under the banner of some distorted form of socialism. Under each government inequality has remained constant, with a powerful white and light-skinned elite exploiting the black majority. Real socialism is as far away as it ever was, and many ghetto "sufferers" still hold the belief that genuine socialism will provide the only answer for the black majority on the island. Linton Kwesi Johnson has pointed out that "the poetry of Jamaican music 'mirrors' the ideological and cultural dimension of class struggle in Jamaica." Obviously, he argues, the Rastafarian cultural consciousness is more in tune with what people in the ghettos want, while the ruling and emergent classes can indulge in a nationalism that frees them from colonialism as they entrench themselves in positions of superiority.[36] Most of the revolutionary music emanates from those with the most to gain from any change. For them it is a continuation of the centuries of using song to fight for freedom.

Traditional music from the Caribbean has been no less radical than the more recently evolved reggae. Calypso songs from Trinidad deal with exploitation that not only was endemic during slavery but also has been part of black-white relations ever since. The Mighty Sparrow has sung "Capitalism Gone Mad" all over the world and, like Explainer, has always been determined to carry on this calypsonian tradition of chipping away at injustice.[37] Cecil Belton is among the many calypso singers who condemned the inequitable Gairy regime in Grenada before the revolution of 1979, and Peter Radix and Grantis Joseph supported Maurice Bishop and warned Grenadians against being beguiled and duped by Americans eager to intervene and depose the People's Revolutionary Government in their country.[38]

Louise Bennet, guardian of the Jamaican dialect poetry that has been a wellspring of inspiration for recent reggae poets, has said that the ancestors of contemporary Jamaica were "warlike, rebellious, they never took slavery quietly. The drums never stopped beating, the traditional culture was always carried on."[39]

Freedom from colonial rule was sought in mento, blue beat, ska, and rock steady. It was a theme that recurred with regularity in early reggae songs. Justin Hinds and The Dominoes asked how long it would be before people were freed from wicked rulers in "Carry Go Bring Come" in 1967.[40] Bruce Ruffin demanded "Free the People" (*Reggae Greats* SHM 786), and in 1969 Ken Boothe sang of "Freedom Street" and "Drums of Freedom" (*Freedom Street*, Trojan 120, 1975). Laid down with producer Leslie Kong, the up-tempo rhythms and reliable guitar were an effective backdrop for the optimistic lyrics. It was, however, a vague notion of "freedom" that prevailed, and a few years later Boothe seemed to go along with the illusion that it had been attained when Manley's People's National Party gained power in 1972.

A substantial number of reggae artists did accommodate to the system—usually in the expectation of finding advancement within it. In "Illiteracy" Horace Andy (Jamaica Music 1, 1975) believes the Manley government will solve all black people's problems—as does Flic Wilson, who praises Manley as the leader who will go down in history for giving black and white people "a ball" and providing free education for all. Delroy Wilson's "Better Must Come" had provided the inspiration for this song and was used as an official campaign song by Manley.[41] Almost as supportive was Max Romeo's "Socialism Is Love," which extols Democratic Socialism as providing equal rights for everyone, whether weak or strong. The problem created by this song was not the words or the music; it was its misuse as propaganda for the inegalitarian Manley regime, which did not promote real socialism or equality.[42]

In the mid-1970s Keith Hudson, who grew up in the Kingston ghetto, stopped producing other artists, like Big Youth, and used his own material on liberation-oriented albums like *Torch of Freedom*.

Having spent time in London and New York, Hudson sees the black struggle as worldwide. Yet he talks more about black control than he does about revolution or equality. Ultimately he seems to be aiming at a black takeover rather than any basic change in the way government and the economy function.[43]

Tapper Zukie was among those who had long had a low opinion of the contemporary political system in Jamaica, and a worse one of the individuals who make politics their career:

None of them is for the people. They just crawl on people's back [sic]. Sucking the people's blood like a vampire. To get rich. . . . The only way it's going to get better is if the youth stop shooting each other and shoot some of the . . . ministers instead.

He went on to say that it was better to kill off two dozen rather than have hundreds dead. He hoped that such minimal violence would prevent a continuation of the divide-and-rule policy that had kept corrupt officials in power. When united, people could take power for themselves. Tapper Zukie is unafraid of the repercussions of singing about such radical policies. He believes it has to be done and is worth any cost to achieve it.[44]

To Joe Higgs, "Every Jamaican government has been the poor man's enemy. Colonialism still exists." For years he has been bitter about the endless arrests and imprisonment of innocent people with no money, while those who are wealthy can commit crimes and go unpunished. He also denounced the inordinate extremes of wealth and poverty, and the exploitation practiced by the middle classes. He challenged this pattern in "Burning Fire," "The World Is Upside Down," "Wave of War," and "Let Us Do Something." Higgs has long been one of the most talented singer-songwriters in Jamaica. He has been in the business since 1958 and helped inspire the young Bob Marley. To him music has to be about "protest," "because I can't sing that things are all right when it's not alright. I sing about reality and try to make the song have a wide scope. I don't write for Jamaicans especially. I write because I'm a poor man. And what I see, the poor man, whether in Vietnam or America or Africa, will have the same understanding." He felt deeply, in the mid-1970s, that "Irrespective of the colour of a man's skin, the most important thing right now is that richer countries supposed to do more work for the small and underdeveloped countries."[45]

The young singer that Joe Higgs once aided was to prove the most determinedly revolutionary, as well as the most successful, reggae star ever to come out of Jamaica. Bob Marley, Bunny Wailer (Neville Livingstone), and Peter Tosh formed The Wailers in the mid-1960s and, under Higgs's direction, began to sing songs that reflected the need for fundamental political and socioeconomic change. They also sang love songs and became popular as rounded artists who reflected every aspect of life. Their album *Soul Rebel* (*Rasta Revolution* in England; Trojan TRLS 89, 1969) became a rallying cry for the disaffected urban youth of Jamaica. The composition of The Wailers changed, but Marley went on singing revolutionary songs throughout the 1970s. In "One Day" on *Survival* (Island ILPS 9542) he sang of the daily need "to keep on fighting." He warned manipulative politicians in "Ambush," on the same album, that while they were fighting for power, the people would rise up against them.

Understanding the role of his music in arousing mass action, Marley called one number "Redemption Song" (*Uprising*, Island ILPS 9596), and warned in "We and Them" that someone would have to pay for the spilling of so much innocent blood. Saba Saakana said of Bob Marley, "Marley is the only artist I know who has been accepted as a commercial proposition by the international market while severely criticizing the system that he operates in." He managed to maintain his rebel stance in spite of his success.[46]

Once Bunny Wailer and Peter Tosh left The Wailers they made some of the toughest musical statements of the 1970s. Bunny Wailer made eloquent musical bids for real freedom and equality on his impressive albums *Blackheart Man* (ILPS 9415, 1976) and *Protest* (ILPS 9512, 1978). They fused hard rhythms with menacing lyrics and acted as a shock treatment for inertia. Peter Tosh came over as even more of a political radical on songs like "Equal Rights," "Get Up, Stand Up," and "Downpressor Man" (*Equal Rights*, Virgin V2081, 1977). In song and in speech he denounced Manley and Seaga as upholders of a corrupt system that sought to exploit the masses for the benefit of the few.

During the Manley and Seaga regimes, a plethora of groups and individuals talked of striving for change. Among them were The Royals urging "People Get Ready" (*Israel Be Wise*, United Artists UAG 30206), The Abyssinians claiming "This Land Is for Everyone"

(*Arise*, Front Line FL 1019, 1978), The Heptones, joyfully proclaiming the imminent arrival of "Better Days" (*Better Days*, Third World TDWD1), and the Gladiators singing of "Struggle" (*Naturally*, Front Line, FL1035, 1979). Earlier, The Pioneers were urging people to join the "Freedom Train" (*Freedom Feeling*, Trojan, 1974), while Roy Cousins and Jah Ted stressed the urgency of "freedom" and "justice" for the people (*Rasta Cry*, Living Music, 1974).

I-Roy and Jazzbo were among those who specifically condemned the exploitation upon which capitalism is based and called for its replacement with a real socialist system.[47] Ijahaman and Burning Spear (Winston Rodney) have persistently called for a war of liberation to bring about a system that will end injustice and establish living conditions appropriate to the natural dignity of man.[48] In a parallel way the Mighty Diamonds sang in 1976 "Go Seek Your Rights" (*Mighty Diamonds*, Right Times Virgin 2052). In this Channel 1 recording with Sly Dunbar as one of the three drummers and Robbie Shakespeare as one of the two bassists, the heavy, insistent rhythm backs up Donald Sharp's persuasive lyrics that urge people to seek their rights—without violence if possible, but with force and the help of the Lord if there is no alternative.

For Black Uhuru, whose very name means "freedom," the revolutionary impulse is as natural as breathing or singing. They extol the virtues of "Solidarity" to overthrow exploitation and talk of a "Right Stuff" combination to go for what people really want. With the emphatic echo of a backing vocoder, revolution is seen as the only solution for the "sufferer" (*Black Uhuru*, Island IRG13, 1985). In 1982 Johnny Osborne, a Kingston reggae star, made an album backed by Roots Radics and produced by Junjo Lawes at Channel 1. *Never Stop Fighting* (Greensleeves GREL 38) was a stomping remorseless plea for real freedom. At much the same time Lloyd Coxone talked on *King of Dub Rock Part 2* (Regal RLP001) of "Black Wars Reggae" and an end to this continuing "Poor Man's Story." Papa Michigan and General Saint rallied black people to alter their repressed condition in "Come on, Black People" (*Downpression*, Greensleeves GREL42, 1985), while Frankie Paul advocated uprising at the "right time."[49]

Eek-a-Mouse, less well known by his real name of Ripton Joseph Hylton, has been described as the "Al Jarreau of reggae and the Gil Scott-Heron of Jamaica." Undoubtedly he also wants radical change so that people can have the work they need, as well as "a good standard of education and decent housing."[50] Far more extreme than Eek-a-Mouse is Mutabaruka, whose razor-sharp poems over a heavy rhythm leave no room for doubt that revolution must be worked toward as the only way injustice and discrimination will be ended.[51]

That this revolution will involve wholesale violence is made clear by Junior Delgado on "I'm Tipping" (*Raggamuffin Year*, Mango 7, 1986). In a wracked voice he warns of the impending destruction if things go on as they are. The monster rhythm pounds the message more securely into the collective brain of the listeners. A year later he issued the single *Forward Revolution* (Message 1, 1987). Here the lyrics are even more sharply backed by insistent horns and percussion, and a simmering synthesizer that makes the march to "revolution" seem both inevitable and imminent.

There are far fewer black British bands that use reggae as a medium to express the belief that only a revolution will succeed in bringing about black equality. One of the earliest and most successful of British reggae bands, Matumbi, went through several changes of personnel before recording *Seven Seals*. In "Hook Deh" Matumbi warns that the "bad situation" will force people to fight for freedom and cause "destruction."[52]

A uniquely revolutionary record cut in the late 1970s was Linton Kwesi Johnson's *Dread Beat and Blood* (Front Line 1017, 1978). The compelling voice of the poet advocated revolutionary socialism but abhorred violence. The lyrics gained resonance from the wonderful rhythms sent pulsing out by Dennis Matumbi, John Bunny, Floyd Lawson, and Vivien Weathers.

Aswad was one of the most regular members of the Rock Against Racism team and declared itself to be working toward socialist goals. This Ladbroke Grove-based, mainly British-born band have a "heavy" reggae rhythm that gives a roots feel to records that incorporate identifiable elements from jazz-funk. On *Live and Direct* (Island IMA6, 1983) they sing of "Revolution," and almost all their songs have a striving rebellious feel.

In 1978 the dynamic British reggae group Steel Pulse not only was seeking, even predicting, a revolution in Handsworth, their area of Birmingham, but also called an album *Handsworth Revolution* (ILPS 9502, 1978). The music uses a heavy reggae beat to propel the urgent demands for "equality" and "justice" that will be backed up with "ammunition" if it proves necessary:

Dread we are for a cause
Deprived of many things
Experienced phoney laws
Hatred Babylon brings
. . .
We will get stronger
And we will conquer
And forward ever and backward never
Handsworth Revolution.

Misty-in-Roots not only has consistently sung anticapitalist songs, it also has avoided being sucked into that aspect of the music business. Instead they established, at the close of the 1970s, a cooperative label, People Unite, profits from which are shared and no one is exploited. The A single released early in 1987—"Own Them, Control Them"—came off an album, *Earth*, that was three years old, but Misty felt that its message had a strong and real appeal in 1987.[53] It is a message that will not lose its point until the economic and political structures of both Britain and Jamaica undergo radical changes, and it is strengthened by their fresh and different sound.

There are also bands whose claim to be reggae artists is thin. A few, such as View from the Hill, are eager to reasssure anyone wanting to label them as dangerous that "I'm No Rebel." Like Eddy Grant, they hope to succeed in music and have no further need for rebellion or revolution. Other bands, like UB 40 and the now defunct Beat, want equality but hope that it can come with a simple change of government. In "Stand Down Margaret," The Beat assumes that the disappearance of Thatcherism will solve problems of poverty and unemployment. The Specials and Selector, two-tone Coventry ska bands, also have disbanded, but they always seemed to think that the British system needed to undergo radical restructuring.[54] They had much in common with a mid-1980s band called Black Britain, a mainly black, all-British band that is committed to radical socialist politics. Their music is highly danceable, with driving rhythms and memorable melodies. That, however, was not enough in 1986 to get their first single, *Ain't No Rockin' in a Police State*, played on the air—it was too dangerously subversive for the BBC.

A new, two-thirds black British group called Three Wise Men made an incendiary rap record called *Urban Hell*. They come from a South London slum and advise the inhabitants to burn it down, right to the ground. Despite this stand they do not see themselves as a political band. They are speaking to people as individuals, and their message is completely conventional: "You have to work hard, we've had to work fucking hard to get where we are."[55]

The 1980s have also given rise to bands in England that are openly socialist. The members of Mighty Ballistics Hi-Power are dedicated socialists and, alongside mainly white bands like The Redskins, Easterhouse, Fire Next Time, and That Petrol Emotion, tell people to take control over their own lives and return political power to the people themselves.[56] Such radical groups believe that by attacking discrimination both within and without the system, they are helping not only to improve life in immediate ways but also to prepare people whose conditions have been made more tolerable to attempt to introduce an alternative system that will equalize the circumstances and opportunities of different races.

Africa has undergone more fundamental changes than any other continent during the past 30 years or so. Countries like Mozambique and Zimbabwe not only have thrown off colonial domination but also have embarked on adventurous plans to adapt socialism to their own particular needs. In such areas, music played its part in supporting and encouraging revolution. In Zimbabwe, for instance, the liberation songs of Thomas Mapfumo both encouraged and accompanied the replacement of white rule, headed by Ian Smith, with black majority rule, led by Robert Mugabe. The music certainly helped raise political consciousness, and Mapfumo has said that as the struggle for freedom became more intense, his music became more revolutionary. His message rang out loud and clear, though mainly transmitted in his native Shona: "We must topple the government."[57] His music was banned on the radio but continued to exert its influence on records. Since then Mapfumo not only has affected musical patterns and taste in the West but also has made constructive lyrical comments for change of a less dramatic nature within the new and far more egalitarian system.

Songs that come out of areas of Africa still dominated by repressive regimes often have to be guarded in their allusions to revolution. If they were more openly subversive, they might be banned. The same circumstances dictate that English will be used sparingly. English has long been a useful means of cross-tribal or inter-tribal or national communication in a variety of African countries, but its advantages are often outweighed by the fact that it can be understood by the constraining blacks as well as white powers-that-be in countries as capitalistic as Kenya.

One man who is aware that repression is not a white prerogative and refuses to be muzzled by its existence is Fela Anikulapo Kuti. To his biographer Carlos Moore, his music is as innately rebellious and revolutionary as the man himself.[58] In "Sorrow, Tears, and Blood," Fela explores the horrific dimensions of the distortion of democracy in postcolonial Nigeria.[59] By 1983 he was committed to the idea of attempting to run for political office himself and to act as a tool of revolution in returning power to the people once he was elected. When questioned by this author on the kind of government he then envisaged, he said that the decisions would lie with the people themselves.[60]

On *Army Arrangement* (Celluloid Cell 6109, 1985), Fela calls on the African people to rid themselves of power-obsessed politicians and create a goverment based on the wishes and needs of the people. Bill Laswell's funky production may have angered Fela, but it adds impetus to the already powerful fusion of strong words and aggressive horns. This album was released during Fela's imprisonment on a spurious currency-smuggling charge, which left no doubt that the military regime then in power regarded him as a dangerous subversive. The coup in August 1985 led ultimately to Fela's release. Since then it seems somehow more obvious "that he embodies the inherent contradictions of Nigeria which make it so difficult to live in and to govern."[61]

Fela is still a "revolutionary," but he has lost a lot of his appeal to his native Nigerians and his aims are also regarded as highly suspect. He wants power to devolve on the people but has no clear idea of how, or of what that would involve. Moreover, any vague notion of equality is negated by his determination to reduce women to the status of chattels and sex objects. He has no coherent plan for a socialist Nigeria, although he has obvious sympathy for the idea of shared wealth and power. Although he is a delight to interview (even for a woman), has an evident concern for people's welfare, and genuinely rejects the existing corruption and misuse of power, he is not likely to make any real difference to the structure of government in Nigeria. His clarion of "music is the weapon of the future" is heard by thousands but how many respond is a very open question.

Another radical Nigerian with a belief in music as a force for change is Sonny Okosun. He not only sings in English as regularly as in Yoruba, but also has been one of the most adept integrators of traditional Nigerian sounds with those of the West. Nurtured on Elvis Presley, Cliff Richard, and the Beatles, Okosun evolved a fusion of styles he called Ozzidi music. He was highly successful with his themes of liberation and peace but had a major hit only when he recorded a reggae version of the Beatles "Help." Okosun believes that reggae has its origins in Nigerian highlife—as with reggae and blues, the main difference is the modified beat. With his subsequent "reggae" dominated albums, from *Papa's Land* to *Fire in Soweto*, he elaborated on and emphasized the liberation theme that was always close to his heart.[62]

Nigeria is full of highlife musicians who are critical of, but not opposed to, the basic structure of the existing form of government. Typical is Rokafil Jazz, which smashed its way to success with *Sweet Mother* in 1977 and then recorded albums about education and politics in Nigeria. *Music Line* was a subsequent album that demonstrated how it was possible to cut through all the setbacks and difficulties, and become successful in music in Nigeria without any kind of revolution. The leader of the band, the half-Nigerian and half-Cameroonian Prince Nico, has become successful enough to set up his own motel, club, and multitrack studio.

Popular though he is in the West, most of Sunny Ade's even more laid-back brand of juju music is sung in Yoruba. But occasionally these songs of critical pessimism use English as a medium of discontent. Yet it is protest with limited aims and intentions: Sunny Ade only wants to improve life on a day-to-day basis rather than transfer to a more people-centered system. Musicians are as aware as political analysts that strong tribal affiliations and rivalry make the possiblity of the devolution of power to the people more complex in Nigeria than in most other countries.

Another politically oriented Nigerian superstar is Ebenezer Obey, who also sings in English, only occasionally. When he does, the message is as sharp as it is in his native tongue. Obey criticizes and advises existing Nigerian regimes in his songs. He does not advocate revolution, but wants to improve the existing lifestyles in the interests of equity and justice. His music is as adaptable as his words. Traditional juju style is embroidered with Western elements, from the blues guitar licks to the electric bass. It is dignified and appropriate without being too disturbingly disruptive.

Ghana has for some time enjoyed a regime that has been far more egalitarian than any of the autocratic rulers who have dominated Nigeria. The changes in Ghana are the subject of witty appreciation. "Sardonic" could be the best description for "Time Changes," a side-long album track sung partly in English by the Ghanaian Kumapim Royals International Band. Against joyous percussion-based rhythmic undulations, revolutionary change in politics and religion is humorously commented on rather than celebrated or demanded by Ampofo Adjei (*Time Changes*, Brobisco House of Music KBLS 20051).

Mohammed Malcolm Benn and his African Feeling Organization (*African Feeling*, Sterns, STERNS 1001) are a Ghanaian band that sing far more revolutionary songs in English. They are more openly accusatory than the customary elliptical style of many African bands. Against a choppy, persistent guitar and swinging horns, the lyrics condemn repression not in Ghana itself, but in Namibia. They also rail against the misuse of the arms trade to prolong regimes that are clearly not in the interests of the people. This is an album with an international feel to both the music and the lyrics. It is also a demonstration of an altrusim and concern for those in positions of unacceptable powerlessness that is common in African music.

In "Think About the People" (*Osibisa*, MCA-MCG 3508), cut in 1971, Osibisa, the multinationality African band that first really popularized African music in England, suggested that "revolution" might be the only answer to the exploitation, injustice, and racism rife in the world. It was an idea that reached a lot of people as it shot up the British charts. This was a popular album in which political songs could reach people alongside "good time" music. Later the band had successful singles, but the 1976 chart-climbing singles were strictly nonpolitical. By then Osibisa was making "party" music rather than music that could push anyone to think about changing society.

In the music generated by black people elsewhere in the world, there is usually a conscious or implicit acceptance or rejection of the dominant sociopolitical and economic systems. As articulators of group responses and ideas, musicians comment on the opportunities, or lack of them, offered by Western democracy and its Third World counterparts. Enslaved or colonized by Western whites, black people have made persistent efforts to win equal treatment within the confines of Western democracy. Yet there have always been those who have viewed such efforts as hopeless and misguided. The evils of slavery and modern capitalism alike have been condemned as exploitative and inherently discriminatory. Occasionally revolution is alluded to or suggested; more often, some kind of fundamental change is demanded or advocated.

There is no clear divide for many people on this tendentious issue. While some revolutionaries are in no doubt that dramatic change is necessary, and some supporters of the establishment want no change at all, far more people want improvements within the existing framework. In the United States the promise of equality enshrined in the Declaration of Independence has kept hope of working within the system burning bright. Elsewhere the presence or even dominance of black politicians in the highest echelons of government has led to expectations of a fair deal for black people. So far these hopes have had only the most marginal degree of fulfillment.

If conditions are this bad in most countries, what impact can songs possibly have on producing change for the better? As Elaine Brown has said, "Songs will not change the world. People change the world." She is among those who think that political statements made in songs may reach more people than straightforward speeches. It is also possible to be more radical in songs than in speeches without being labeled dangerous. What is said in the songs will have an impact only if it hits a nerve in the listener. If there is a recognition that a song is telling the truth, it may produce a feeling of solidarity and unity. In addition, half-formulated discontent or arguments can be taken to logical conclusions. All of this can be a spur to action and certainly can help create a state of mind conducive to action. In South Africa, more than any other country, the time for extreme action obviously has arrived. There music is being used as external pressure applied to the stubbornly unbending Boer dictatorship, and as sustenance and encouragement to black South Africans who are building a revolution.

NOTES

1. Quoted in David Fenton, ed., *Shots: A Liberation News Source* (London: Academy Editions, 1972), p. 42.

2. "Two Nations Gap Widens," government statistics quoted in *The Guardian*, January 29, 1987, p. 5; M. Davis, Fred Pfeil, and Michael Sprinkler, *The Year Left* (London: Verso, 1985), p. 82.

3. George Breitman, *The Last Years of Malcolm X: The Evolution of a Revolutionary* (New York: Schocken, 1968), p. 19.

4. Huey Newton, quoted in David Fenton, ed., *Shots: Photographs from the Underground Press* (London: Academy Editions, 1972), unpaginated.

5. Quoted in Fenton, *Shots*.

6. Dave Harker and Alan Fair, "U.S. Imperialism and U.S. Popular Music," unpublished paper, p. 25.

7. Lemuel Berry, "The Spiritual: A Rebellious Song," unpublished paper, p. 7.

8. Berry, "Spiritual," p. 10.

9. John Lovell, Jr., *Black Song: The Forge and the Flame, the Story of How the Afro-American Spiritual Was Hammered Out* (New York: Macmillan, 1972), pp. 323, 334, 340.

10. Dena Epstein, *Sinful Tunes and Spirituals* (Urbana: University of Illinois Press, 1977), p. 72.

11. Paul Robeson, *Here I Stand* (New York: Othello Associates, 1958), p. 11; *New York Times*, April 5, 1931.

12. Greil Marcus, *Mystery Train: Images of America in Rock 'n' Roll Music* (New York: Dutton, 1982), p. 23.

13. Louis Jordan, *In Memoriam*, MCA Coral 6.22175 AK; *Choo, Choo Ch' Boogie*, MPF 50557.

14. Various artists, *Harmonicas Unlimited*, Document DLP 503/4 (1986).

15. Juke Boy Bonner, *I'm Going Back to the Country*, Arhoolie F1036 (1968), and *The Struggle*, Arhoolie AR 19002 (1968).

16. Eddie Clearwater, *Two Times Nine*, Charly R&B 1025.

17. *New Musical Express*, April 16, 1985, p. 7.

18. Dave Hill, "The Saving of America's Soul," *The Guardian*, December 27, 1985, p. 7.

19. Harold Melvin and The Blue Notes, *Reaching for the World*, ABC Million Dollar Records AB–969 (1976).

20. Curtis Mayfield, *We're a Winner*, ABC 11022 (1968).

21. "Towards a New Constitution," *The Black Panther* 4, no. 28 (June 13, 1970): centerfold.

22. Archie Shepp, *Poem for Malcolm*, Affinity FA23, (1969).

23. Sly and the Family Stone, *There's a Riot Goin' On*, Epic 30986 (1971); Marcus, *Mystery Train*, pp. 83, 85.

24. Marcus, *Mystery Train*, p. 258.

25. *The Temptations*, EMI/Motown STMX 6002 (1970).

26. "Motown Trackin'" *Blues and Soul*, May 18–31, 1982, p. 16.

27. Nina Simone, *Take Off: Black Soul*, RCA CL42220 (1977).

28. O'Jays, *Travelin' at the Speed of Thought*, Philadelphia International PIR 81977 (1977).

29. Stevie Wonder, *Songs in the Key of Life*, Motown TMSP 6002 (1976), and *Innervisions*, Tamla Motown STMA 8011 (1973).

30. Chris May, "In a Lifeboat," *Black Music and Jazz Review*, September 1983, p. 14.

31. Interview with Gil Scott-Heron, Jubilee Gardens, London, June 2, 1985.

32. David Troop, *The Rap Attack: African Jive to New York Hip Hop* (London: Pluto, 1984), p. 58.

33. Edna Edet, "One Hundred Years of Black Protest Music," *Black Scholar*, July–August 1976, p. 48.

34. Nona Hendrix, *The Heat*, RCA PL 85465 (1985).

35. Amiri Baraka with David Murray and Steve McCall, *New Music— New Poetry*, India Navigation IN–1048 (1981).

36. Linton Kwesi Johnson, "The Politics of the Lyrics of Reggae Music," *The Black Liberator* no. 4 (August 1976): 364.

37. Claire Shepherd, "With His Bow and Arrow," *Black Music and Jazz Review*, June 1983, p. 26; Explainer, *Man from the Ghetto*, Charlies (1982).

38. Polly McLean, "Calypso and Revolution in Grenada," *Popular Music and Society* 10, no. 4 (1986): 87–99.

39. Chris May, "Miss Lou's Views," *Black Music and Jazz Review*, June 1983, p. 22.

40. Sebastian Clarke (Saba Saakana), *Jah Music: The Evolution of Popular Jamaican Song* (London: Heinemann, 1980), p. 91.

41. Flic Wilson, *Free Education for All*, Shelley Music CS 037A (1973); Clark, *Jah Music*, p. 95.

42. Max Romeo, *Socialism Is Love*, Blackword PC 194C 19104.

43. Carl Gaye, "There Is Nowhere I Would Rather Be Than in Rasta Country," *Black Music*, January 1977, pp. 16–19.

44. Chris May, "Ghetto Warrrior," *Black Music*, September 1983, p. 10.

45. Carl Gayle, "Joe Higgs: The Man Who Inspired the Wailers," *Black Music*, October 1975, p. 20; Joe Higgs, *Life of Contradiction*, Grounation, GROL 508 (1975).

46. Clarke, *Jah Music*, p. 116.

47. Clarke, *Jah Music*, pp. 123–124.

48. Burning Spear, *Social Living*, One Stop STOP 1001 (1978), *Man in the Hills*, Island ILPS 9412 (1976), *Dry and Heavy*, Island ILPS 9431 (1977).

49. Papa Michigan and General Saint, *Downpression*, Greensleeves, GREL 42 (1985); Frankie Rich, *Rich and Poor*, Classic (1985).

50. Bob Katz, "Rodent Control," *Black Music and Jazz Review*, November 1983, pp. 14–15.

51. Mutabaruka, *Check It!*, Alligator AL8306 (1983).

52. Matumbi, *Seven Seals*, Harvest SHSP 4090 (1978).

53. Simon Buckland, "Play Misty for Me," *Echoes*, January 17, 1987, p. 18.

54. *The Specials*, 2 Tone/Chrysalis CDLTT 5001 (1979); The Specials, *Ghost Town*, CHSTT 17 (1981); Selector, *Celebrate the Bullet*, 2 Tone/Chrysalis CHR 1306, (1981).

55. Paolo Hewitt, "Wisdom Against Aggression," *The New Musical Express*, October 18, 1986, p. 13.

56. Mighty Ballistics Hi-Power, *here comes the blues*, Criminal Damage CRI MLP 131 (1986).

57. Fred Zindi, *Roots Rocking in Zimbabwe* (Gweru: Mambo Press, 1985), p. 34.

58. Carlos Moore, *Fela, Fela—This Bitch of a Life* (London: Allison and Busby, 1982), p. 12.

59. Fela Anikulapo Kuti, *Black President*, Arista Spart 1167 (1981).

60. Interview with Fela Kuti, London: December 12, 1983.

61. John Howe, "Fela Kuti," *The Guardian*, September 26, 1985, p. 25.

62. John Collins, *African Pop Roots: The Inside Rhythms of Africa*, (London: W. Foulsham and Co. Ltd., 1985), pp. 43–45.

4   *Liberation Songs for South Africa*

However great the need for change elsewhere, it is South Africa that has caused the greatest anger in the hearts and minds of anyone concerned with freedom and equality. No other country has consistently denied both, in such a flagrant and consistent way, to the majority of its own people. The removal of basic human rights has been so absolute for so many people that the sense of outrage has sent shock waves around the world. This outrage has been compounded by a need to support the black resistance that has been gaining strength ever since apartheid became the official policy of the South African government after 1948. Riding against the international tide of gradual desegregation, South Africa imposed a rigid and formal code of total separation on its black majority. Dutch colonialism in South Africa was always highly exploitative; the extent of the denial of black rights became obvious when the British took over in 1815 and attempted to introduce some justice for the black people who had been oppressed for over 150 years. The British also aroused Boer hatred by attempting to seize effective control of those areas where gold could be mined. The uneasy truce of the Act of Union in 1910, which gave South Africa "self-government," led to the Natives Land Act, which prohibited native South Africans from buying or living on 93 percent of the nation's land. The pattern of herding black people onto reserves where they could be drawn on as pools of migrant labor was established.

European colonization had been exploitive and unjust throughout Africa; but, just at the time when other countries were successfully claiming their independence and either fighting for or establishing black majority rule, an oppressive system of apartheid was being established in South Africa. Instead of acquiring more power and freedom, black South Africans were shunted into "homeland" areas or townships where opportunities for economic advancement were few. Black people were denied the minimal democratic right of voting, and were subjected to humiliation and degradation in order to keep them separate and inferior. The architect of apartheid was the Nazi-educated Hendrik F. Verwoerd, who reduced the already limited education and opportunities open to black people and removed any necessity for segregated families to be equal. The accumulated restrictions resulted in black resistance, and in 1960, 69 black South Africans were shot at Sharpeville.

Despite Verwoerd's assassination in 1966, the policy of segregating most black people into arid "homelands" was carried through. Rioting broke out in 1976 in Soweto and elsewhere, focusing on the introduction of Afrikaans as a teaching medium. The following year Steve Biko, leader of the Black Consciousness movement that gave birth to the socialist Azanian movement, was killed while in police custody. Black resistance grew stronger as "reforms" of a pathetic and minimal nature were introduced by Prime Minister Botha after 1978.

Real practical resistance to apartheid (pronounced "apart-hate," according to the Washington office of the Africa Educational Fund) came early from black south Africans. The African National Congress (ANC) was formed in 1912, but it was during and after the 1960s that it really began organizing opposition. Its most renowned member, Nelson Mandela, was arrested in 1962 for calling a strike (as well as for leaving the country without a passport) and has been imprisoned ever since. The Azanian movement sprang out of Black Consciousness and has recently marshaled support for a socialist South Africa. The Pan-African Congress was always opposed to any collaboration with whites, and from the early 1960s adopted a white assassination policy. Since the early 1980s the United Democratic Front has acted as a "confederation" or front for over 600 banned organizations. It also has encouraged the township violence against black collaborators with the government.

Since the 1950s and 1960s, apartheid has been so solidly opposed by the indigenous population that a cohesive grass-roots movement for a socialist South Africa has developed. Students and trade union-ists, people who live in the homelands, and those who are based in the townships, want a complete transformation of the inequitable capi-talist system. They are aware that racism is a side effect of capitalism and are working through organizations like the Azanian movement and the ANC for its overthrow. The Azanian movement is totally committed to socialism and has a more coherent political philosophy, while the ANC contains within its ranks those who would retain capitalism as well as those who are avowed Communists.

Saths Cooper, a leading exponent of Black Consciousness in the 1980s and a former vice-president of Azanian People's Organization (Azapo), who is now in the United States, has a perfectly clear view of the whole problem: "We basically analyse the problem as one constituted by racism and capitalism; there is an amalgam, the one bolsters the other. The solution to that problem can never come from within the ranks of that problem."[1]

Azapo, whose motto is "One People, One Nation," and whose emblem is the clenched fist of solidarity, reemphasized in 1986 that the existing economic and political system must be fought by every means possible. To this end its members work as individuals to politicize and activate groups and communities, and use appropriate "freedom songs" to emphasize and give popular expression to their ideals.

The current chairperson of the Black Consciousness Movement of Azania, Mosibudi Mangena, pointed out at the end of 1986:

The struggle in Azania [South Africa] is not an anti-apartheid one, for apartheid is only a superficial manifestation of the essence of our oppres-sion. The problem in Azania is white racist settler-colonialism. The whites stole our land in 1652 and called it their own. Our struggle is therefore to reconquer our land and restore it to its rightful owners, and we SHALL GET OUR LAND BACK. . . . White folks can only become Azanians through baptism by the fire of black revolution and freedom.[2]

He went on to say that there was a huge army of untrained Azanians willing to fight for socialism and freedom without further delay.

The proliferation of freedom songs within South Africa is one example of the growth in strength of collective resistance. Most of these songs are sung in tribal languages like Zulu or Xhosa, but some are in English. Once elliptical or ironic, such songs have become increasingly straightforward in their warnings of violence and upheaval. Women sing of their aroused strength as a boulder pushed to the brink that will crush the oppressor with its size and weight. In these songs the collective desire for total transformation of the way in which South Africa is run and governed is glaringly obvious.

Song has been seen as "dangerous" by the South African government. Oscar Mpeta, an aging trade unionist, is among those who have been imprisoned for singing "subversive" songs. Rufus Radebe and Joseph Charles, two young musicians who sang about Nelson Mandela, were imprisoned for two and four years, respectively. James Mahhlope Phillips has been arrested several times not only for singing but also for organizing and encouraging people with song in strikes and protests.

Phillips sings both traditional songs and new songs, and has recently concentrated on songs spawned by the accelerating struggle for freedom. He

illustrates in word and song what it is that the people of South Africa want and how the songs have become more determined and defiant over the years, indicating that the people are no longer patiently awaiting change but willing to fight for it. The songs, he says, are a part of the armoury of our people, they are marching side by side with them, they are a way of life.[3]

Violence has been an inevitability in South Africa. The more violence has been unreasonably directed against the suffering black population, the more it has become justifiably directed against the white oppressors. Some reports have it that 10,000 children and students marched in Soweto in 1976 and almost 1,400 were massacred, detonating a new stage in the "struggle for national liberation."[4] Violence is now more than a defensive weapon for black people; it has finally become a force for change of the most fundamental kind.

South African poets acknowledge the primacy of music and violence in the struggle. Lindiwe Mabuza expects freedom to be reached while marching

> To the unbroken rhythm
> Of surging, dancing spears,

and Victor Matlou anticipates that hope will "breathe songs" into the hearts of those selflessly dedicated to the cause. Poet and revolutionary activist Keorapetse Kgositsile praises the music of groups like

Juluka, Sakhile, and the Malopoets for making "their art functional in the needs and interests of the people." They are seen to be demonstrating revolutionary cohesiveness in the battle for national liberation.[5]

Juluka is not alone in risking censure and more for daring to be a mixed-race band in segregated South Africa, but its visibility has always been high on the "free" concert circuit and through albums like *Scatterlings* (Shaka 1). It has been more extreme in its criticism of the Botha regime and its advocacy of violent resistance in recent live performances. In mid-1986 Juluka disbanded (with some commitment to future recording precluding any funeral rites). Some members of the band have re-formed as Savuka (Zulu for "we are rising"), and their spokesman, Johnny Clegg, has said, "It is important that musicians now align themselves with progressive political forces." To him, "There is a positive role musicians can play" as part of a liberation culture that is emerging all over the world.[6]

What South African poet Dennis Brutus has called "the lust for freedom" burns as strongly in verses that are sung as any that are printed or read as poems.[7] Township bands have sung constantly of freedom, and The Mahotella Queens and Ladysmith Black Mambazo are among those that on rare occasions sing in English of the need to seize that long denied liberty. One South African writer has said, "Songs are part and parcel of the struggle for freedom and are significant historical documents."[8]

The South African government became more and more determined to remove even the freedom to sing or play jazz of a subversive nature, and many of the more harassed musicians felt they had no option but to leave their country and fight the system from outside. Among those who fled initially to the United States were Miriam Makeba, Hugh Masekela, and Abdullah Ibrahim (Dollar Brand). They had all become dangerous because they were regarded as local heroes who were dedicated to giving substantial support to the swelling revolutionary impulse.

In South Africa, as early as the 1960s, there no longer seemed any point in attempting to accommodate to such a totally reprehensible, repressive system. Miriam Makeba insists that she is not a political singer; she just tells the truth about the situation in South Africa. Anyone who tells the truth also advocates complete change and removal of oppression. In South Africa that is undoubtedly revolutionary. Her resonating voice soars and bends as she sings of change and release from oppression in English as well as her native Xhosa.

In 1987 Ladysmith Black Mambazo, Hugh Masekela, and Miriam Makeba all appeared with Paul Simon on his Graceland tour. A storm of controversy was caused by the record that preceded the tour. The record broke the "sanctions" ban on Western artists working in South Africa. The artists involved did gain publicity and some of the profits, but it was undoubtedly the career and pocket of Paul Simon that benefited most. The previously unsullied reputations of Masekela, Makeba, and Ladysmith became tainted with opprobrium, and to many, including the ANC, it seemed that they had hampered, rather than enhanced, the cause of freedom in South Africa.

Abdullah Ibrahim was originally known as Dollar Brand and played good time jazz in his native South Africa. Now those who hear his music have a different sort of good time, sharing music that is a spiritual experience and is alive with the vitality of fused cultures. Jazz itself is a uniquely American mix of African and European music in which the African element is clearly dominant. Abdullah infuses jazz with its roots when he plays delicate, almost classical sequences of notes on his solo piano introductions to pieces that become dominated by urgent African rhythms and harmonies. Yet the eclectic sounds form a perfectly integrated whole, as becomes a musician who owes a special debt to Duke Ellington, and who has lived and worked in the United States since the late 1960s. Most members of Ekaya, his talented band, are American, but the massed horns of Carlos Ward (flute and soprano sax), Ricky Ford (tenor sax), Charles Davis (baritone sax), and Dick Griffin (trombone) create an authentic South African pattern and spirit.

Abdullah Ibrahim, born in Cape Town, makes clear and informed anti-apartheid statements in his music. "Soweto," "Mandela," and "The River" are anthems to the spirit of resistance that is guiding black South Africans to seek equality and justice. It seems perfectly natural to him that music should accompany and spur on the struggle, since "the whole of Africa moves in time to music." He does not venture to assume that the contained passion of his music can change hearts and minds, but says simply, "I want people to get from my music whatever they feel they can accept."[9] Hearing such music, few people could remain unmoved or untouched.

In the United States, Hugh Masekela not only won an admirable reputation as a versatile but distinctive trumpeter with a decidedly South African feel, he also produced a seminally revolutionary

album, *Colonial Boy*. Here all the pent-up frustration of the colonization and exploitation of his ancestors and countrymen poured out.
Anger reverberated through his attacking lyrics and ice-cold notes
that dropped from his finely controlled horn. Over the last few years
he has played many anti-apartheid benefits both in the United States
and England, and in 1987 he produced an album called *Tomorrow*
(WEA 2545731), on which he once again took on the corrupt and
inequitable South Africa regime. If his joyous, attacking music is
premonitory, victory is certain.

Exiled South African bands in England have been using music in
the battle against apartheid since the early 1970s. Dudu Pukwana has
been at the forefront of this movement. Through the varied sounds of
bands from Assegai and Spear of Destiny to Zila, he has pursued the
elusive dream of equality for black people in South Africa.[10] Like
Julian Bahula, he has used England as his base since the early 1970s.
Julian Bahula has been the most significant organizer of musical
activities that are designed to promote fundamental change in South
Africa. Not only has he led an impressive African band, Julian
Bahula's Jabula, more or less since his arrival in Britain in 1973, he
also has untiringly organized benefits to attract sympathy and funds
to the black South African cause. He writes rousing lyrics telling
people to "wake up" and act.[11] In the spring of 1987 Bahula was as
active as ever, arranging, among many other events, a benefit night
for SACTU (South African Congress of Trade Unions) at which his
own Electric Dream band headlined.

Both Dudu Pukwana and Julian Bahula have always made joyous,
positive music. It is not music of despair or resentment; it is music of
hope and determination. It is so life affirming that the horns and
percussion are as much a call to action as the voices and the words.
Dudu Pukwana said, in interviews with this author in the spring of
1985 and the summer of 1987, that music is a powerful force for
change. All Julian Bahula's campaigns and compositions are based
on that assumption; this quiet, gentle man has changed many hearts
and minds over the years and has provided financial aid to black
movements within South Africa.

One of the benefits Bahula organized at Alexandra Palace in the
summer of 1984 brought together several South African and African
musicians in a spectacular concert that was then issued on record.
Hugh Masekela joined forces with Orchestra Jazira and Bahula's
Jazz Afrika to create *African Sounds for Mandela* (Tsafrika TSA

1003, 1984). Julian Bahula paid a moving tribute to the imprisoned ANC martyr in "Mandela," and Masekela was as effective as a vocalist as he was as a trumpeter on "Bajabula" and "Stimela." The staccato sax of Dudu Pukwana gave the record an inimitable style and feel.

One of the most talented of South Africa's exiles, Chris Mac-Gregor is a charming, unassuming white South African who speaks with confident expectation of liberation as a spiritual and physical human right. He can be heard not only with his own mainly black band, The Brotherhood of Breath, but also on District 6's 1987 album *To Be Free* and live with bands, such as Dudu Pukwana's Zila, whose ethos and music are directed toward freedom for both expatriates and those still living under the flattening iron of apartheid.

Amandla was a record and a collection of songs and theater sketches performed by the cultural branch of the ANC in various countries. The songs attack the murder and injustice prevalent in South Africa in the 1980s. Whether on record or on stage in Britain and elsewhere, the songs aroused indignation and empathy. The group is not exiled, just touring. In a similar way theater groups have taken songs from South Africa around other countries as integral aspects of plays. Poppie Nongena and Woza Albert had several mildly liberationist songs in their repertoires. *Burning Embers*, and the Azanian theater production, goes much further, and is entirely revolutionary in its basic plot, performance, and songs. These are so wrenchingly realistic and truthful that they are a definite call to action of the most compelling kind.

Kintone is a younger South African band that has used England as a recording base in the mid-1980s. On its album *Going Home* (Sterns 1013, 1985) they not only sing "Freedom's Song" but also look forward to a postrevolutionary situation. On their 12-inch single *State of Emergency* (KMC01, 1986) they stress the desperation of the present situation, and on the sleeve say that people in South Africa "live in a permanent state of emergency." They list the brutality and murders, the imprisonment, torture, and death that are common, and add: "As history records the aspirations of our people, it will be the strength and defiance, the courage and the sacrifices which will prove that with justice on our side *the spirit of freedom cannot be crushed.*"

The oppression of black people in South Africa has aroused world-wide anger, and expression of this anger in song has come from countries near and far. The very nearest is obviously Lesotho, which is virtually an island stranded in the middle of South Africa. Sankomota is a band from Lesotho that is clearly opposed to the puppet government installed by South African fascists. It has produced a stirring, thoughtful, action-inducing album that was recorded in the mobile Shifty Studio. Its complex set of musical patterns ranges from traditional South African rhythms and polyrhythms to a beat that borders on reggae, and its lyrics are equally eclectic. The members sing in English, Sotho, and a kind of Zulu used in Lesotho. In "Vukani" they urge people to awake from their untimely sleep and get themselves together. They urge people to stop distracting themselves with drink or drugs, and start to use their brains and their united force to change things. Another track, "House on Fire," is related like a dream where suddenly there is fire, but to combat it, it is necessary to use "a shield and a spear." The image is one of an incendiary revolution rather than a domestic fire. Throughout the album, the most frequently recurring word is "freedom"—and this is an album filled with its very essence. Yet it is an album that only marginally reflects the fury that is generated in and about South Africa itself.[12]

Other expressions of African solidarity with the freedom fight in South Africa have come from Nigeria's Sonny Okosun with his powerful "Fire in Soweto." This has been sung live as well as on record since the early 1980s, and more recently anti-apartheid records have proliferated all over the continent. One of the more unusual was released by the Ivory Coast musician Alpha Blondy. Like Okosun, he uses reggae as his musical medium, but the overall interaction of the horns and percussion as they dance around the reggae beat is fresh and original. The lyrics declare that "Apartheid is Nazism" and call on America to "break the neck" of the iniquitous system. Blondy adds, "black and white, we are all the same" and no one should be able to behave like Hitler in 1985.[13]

Kaleidoscopic African sounds are used by some musicians to reinforce the anti-apartheid messge. Yousson N'Dour draws on the music of diverse African traditions in his 1986 album *Nelson Mandela*, while Mwana Musa uses the massed African and Caribbean talent of his English-based band, African Connection, to urge freedom for Nelson Mandela and all black South Africans.

One of the most brilliant records to come out of England in the early 1980s was Special AKA's "Free Nelson Mandela." This anthemic yet uncluttered song, by the black and white band that had emerged from the ashes of The Specials, has been sung live all around the world as an indictment of South Africa's blatant disregard for justice. Another politically motivated black and white band, Latin Quarter, had a hit in 1985 with "Radio Africa," in which a heavy bass line echoed the lyrics that called the South African government a "monster" and urged on the socialist movement in southern Africa.[14] Labi Siffre's "So Strong," a 1987 plea for an end to apartheid, is less sophisticated but packs a melodic and lyrical punch that makes it no less effective.

British reggae bands like Steel Pulse have long been concerned with their "brothers in south of Afrika" (*Handsworth Revolution*, Island ILPS 9502, 1978). In 1985 this simple solidarity on one album track turned into a far more complicated and intense desire to help defeat those who would turn people into martyrs (*Tribute to the Martyrs*, Mango MLPs 9568).

West Indian singers were equally determined to use music as a weapon to defeat apartheid. Peter Tosh insisted in 1977 that people must "fight, fight, fight, against apartheid" (*Equal Rights*, Virgin V2081), and at about the same time The Abyssinians put their compelling rhythm and melodies to good use, giving "South African Enlistment" a musical cutting edge.[15] Mutabaruka was the clearest voice among those who argued that they could not be free if South Africa was suffering.[16] By 1986 apartheid was being attacked on countless records, from Junior Murvin's *Apartheid* through Johnny Osborne's *Wipe Out Apartheid* to Mighty Sparrow's incendiary calypso *Invade South Africa*.[17]

At Toronto's annual West Indian carnival or Caribana, a steel band that had frequently won the main carnival contest decided to show their support for black South Africa. In 1985 Afropan made its aims clear: by assuming the garb of prisoners and playing appropriate music, they wanted "everyone to remember the suffering. It is youth here supporting youth in South Africa. We want to make a political statement rather than just going down the road having a good time." Some people opposed them for making Caribana political, but others replied that West Indian music was almost always political, and this was an opportunity to use music to draw attention to racism in the music industry and in Canada, as well as in South Africa.[18]

The idea of music as a medium for effective protest was singularly alive in Toronto. The Black Music Association (BMA) had censured all those artists who had performed in Sun City and had staged protests in front of the South African Embassy in the city. As a direct result of these protests there was a flood of anti-apartheid records, including those by the vocal calypso star Jayson (*Free South Africa*, JBS Records, LL1005A, 1985) and the reggae singer Xola (*South Africa*, Rebel Radio, 1986). The BMA was committed to a demonstration of solidarity with black South Africans: "Globally we will all be free together or we will not be free at all." Dick Griffey, chairman of the BMA, said in 1985: "It's time for this industry to stand up. We have power through our communications. And through our communications we can educate. We can't sit back and let Margaret Thatcher or Ronald Reagan tell us what to do about apartheid." He wanted people to be able to say that "the Black Music Association, and the music industry were instrumental in being on the right side of morality, on the right side of justice."[19]

Pefectly sensibly, Pauline Haslebacher preceded her analysis of anti-apartheid steel band music in Toronto with the question "What effects will the efforts of the black music community in Canada, let alone the steel band community in Toronto, have on the Apartheid regime in South Africa?" Salim Vally, a member of the South Africa Black Consciousness Movement in Johannesburg, had addressed this question in a keynote speech at the Issues for the Next Generation conference held in Toronto, August 17–21, 1985:

Our struggle is a universal struggle. In South Africa it may be more brutal, but it is an international struggle against exploitation and oppression. Our culture is a culture of resistance; we have nothing to lose and all to gain. It is not sufficient for culture to reflect an awareness of oppression and exploitation; such awareness only becomes meaningful when it leads to action to end that oppression. In this sense, culture is a weapon in our struggle; it is a tool to build a new society. All efforts, whether they be on an individual, group, or national level, to raise public awareness of our struggle will help in seeking action on a government level.[20]

The country that was to make the greatest concerted effort to really affect the South African situation through music was, of course, the United States with the recording of *Sun City*. There was a long background of anti-apartheid numbers that had been released by black activist musicians in the United States. One of the first was Max Roach's classic "Tears of Johannesburg," recorded as early as 1961. Among the more renowned songs that followed was Gil Scott-

Heron's rousing call for support for black brothers in or near "Johannesburg" (Arista 0152, 1975): "they need to know we're on their side."

Another of the most urgent calls to action came from Sweet Honey in the Rock, singing a powerful a cappella song for the freedom of black South Africans. In "Azanian Freedom Song" (*We All Every One of Us*, Spindrift SPIN 106, 1983) the deaths of Steve Biko and too many black children are mourned, and the imminent arrival of real "freedom" is heralded.

A more obtuse but musically unnerving attack on apartheid pounded out from the astringent "Rock This House" (*The Heat*, RCA PL85465, 1985), written and sung by Nona Hendryx. She demanded an end to a world that can allow millions of hungry people, one where "the good life is still exclusive." More direct was Stevie Wonder's "It's Wrong (Apartheid)."[21] In some of the most agitatory lyrics he has written, Wonder condemns the atrocity of the South African system as equatable with slavery, and too evil for even the devil to approve. He has no doubt that "freedom is coming" and "the whole world is with us." He backed his words with action when he organized anti-apartheid concerts and was arrested in 1985 for demonstrating outside the South African Embassy in Washington. In 1987 he reinforced this with his outspoken "Dark 'n' Lovely" on his *Characters* album. He condemns with disgust the way apartheid turns children into terrorists.

Sun City itself was quintessentially a collaboration of music and action. It was a marshaling of ideas and personalities, of music and the music industry to represent the situation in South Africa accurately and help to change it. This was not another Band Aid, because it was not only intended to provide funds for the black South African struggle; it was meant to be part of the fight. It was an act of confrontation and solidarity. The South African government was challenged, and black South Africans were given total sympathy and support.

The whole affair was originated, the song was written, by Little Steven, but he used mainly black artists to sing the resounding words. With stark clarity they argue that now is the time for justice and truth, and that the homelands are "phoney." All the singers keep repeating that none of them will play Sun City. The song opens with an angry trumpet obbligato by Miles Davis and is taken up by rappers Run-DMC, Melle Mel, Afrikaa Bambaataa, and Kurtis Blow. Later the sentiments are driven home by reggae stars Big Youth, Jimmy Cliff, and Linton Kwesi Johnson. Soul singers David Ruffin, Eddie Kendricks, and Bobby Womack come in to denounce South African policies and American silence while a battery of rock singers from Nona Hendryx to Bono throw in reinforcements of fact and feelings. The music is fired by a sense of disgust at the atrocities perpetrated in South Africa by the white ruling elite.[22] The record and video have been widely used in the United States as educational tools. Schools study the song and the horrors of South African racism through an educational pack, and teachers are provided with accurate information and coherent ideas to help them explain the reality and the song. The *Sun City* record uses the words and music of the song as a weapon in the fight to persuade people of the evils of apartheid and of the necessity of at least imposing a total boycott and tight sanctions.

In very specific terms the record is intended to expose the fact that Sun City is an artificial showcase for white visitors placed in the middle of the poverty-striken "homeland" of Bopthuthatswana. It highlights the determination of the white regime to increase the already grinding poverty of black South Africans by pushing them against their will into such theoretically "independent" areas. The musicians who took part in the recording of *Sun City* were equally committed to exposing this exploitation and the obscenity of placing a city of such wealth in an area of such poverty and claiming it was an integrated city. They wanted it more widely known that South Africa's white minority of 16 percent of the population (4.5 million) owns or controls 87 percent of the land, while the 84 percent who are black (20 million), colored (2.8 million), or Indian (0.9 million) are shunted onto the most barren 13 percent of their own territory. Once these bantustan "homelands" are declared independent (as four had been by the mid-1980s), their inhabitants lose their South African citizenship and have no claim politically or economically on the land that is rightfully theirs.

This record is meant to catalyze revolt, and one of the tracks on the album is totally unambivalent about its role. "Revolutionary Situations" features the voices of Prime Minister Botha, Ronald Reagan, Bishop Desmond Tutu, and Nelson Mandela—as well as those of randomly selected South Africans. A rare tape of Mandela, made in 1961, was found in London and used on the track, so that all those people who venerated him but had never heard his voice would at last have him on record. Almost equally unexpected is the voice of Miles

Davies spontaneously rapping on this track in between his own trumpet solos, chanting by The Malopoets, and fragments of the outlawed national anthem of black South Africa, "Nkosi Sikelela Afrika."

The hope was that this multiracial collaborative record, by focusing on racism in South Africa, would simultaneously draw attention to American racism. It was a record that could not help but provoke thought and alter those minds open to any kind of persuasion. The money it raised was of immense value, but it was its role as a musical force for change that was fundamentally more essential.

On records like *Sun City*, and so many others, even singers of moderate political persuasion support the idea of revolution. It is evident that in South Africa equality will be won only by a complete overturning of the system that has for so long proved so reliant on the misuse of black labor for white profit and the misappropriation of black lands for white use. In such circumstances, music is a weapon in the armory of revolutionary change.

NOTES

1. Julie Frederikse, *South Africa: A Different Kind of War* (Gweru: Mambo Press, 1986), p. 37.

2. Mosibundi Mangena, "Speech Delivered at the Third Malhaba Conference in Tripoli," *Solidarity: Official Organ of the Black Consciousness Movement of Azania* no. 13 (December 1986): 13–15.

3. A. Siemsen, "Anthems of Freedom," *Third World Book Review* 2, nos. 1 and 2 (1986): 105.

4. Jean Damu, "South Africa: From Angola to Soweto," *Black Scholar*, September 1976, p. 9.

5. Keorapetse Kgositsile, "Language as a Weapon in the Struggle," *Third World Book Review* 2, nos. 1 and 2 (1986): 103–104.

6. Extract from *Vula* magazine, quoted in *Africa Beat* no. 5 (Summer 1986): 13.

7. Dennis Brutus, "Untitled," *Black Scholar*, January/February 1978, p. 35.

8. Siemsen, "Anthems," p. 105.

9. Interview by this author with Abdullah Ibrahim at Sweet Basil's, New York City, August 14, 1986.

10. Assegai, *Afro-Rock*, EMI SPR 90054 (1971).

11. Julian Bahula, *Jabula*, JBL 2002 (1979).

12. *Sankomota*, Earthworks ELP 2007 (1985).

13. Alpha Blondy, *Apartheid Is Nazism*, Sterns 1017 (1986).

14. Latin Quarter, *Modern Times*, Rocking Horse/Arista RHLPI (1985).

15. The Abyssinians, *Arise*, Front Line FL 1019 (1978).

16. Mutabaruka, *Check It!*, Alligator AL 8306 (1983).

17. Junior Murvin, *Apartheid*, Greensleeves GREL 95 (1986); Mighty Sparrow, *Invade South Africa*, BT Records BSRSP 041 (1986).

18. Pauline Haslebacher, "Political Activism in the Toronto Steel Band Community: The Use of Music as a Tool in the Struggle Against Apartheid," paper presented at the Joint American Culture Association/Popular Culture Association Conference in Atlanta, Georgia, April 2–6, 1986, pp. 8–11.

19. Haslebacher, "Toronto," p. 8.

20. Haslebacher, "Toronto," p. 1.

21. Stevie Wonder, *In a Square Circle*, Motown 2L72205 (1985).

22. Artists United Against Apartheid, *Sun City*, Manhattan Records MTL 1001 (1985): Dave Marsh, *Sun City by Artists Against Apartheid: The Making of the Record* (Harmondsworth: Penguin, 1985).

5 *Freedom Is a Lonely Word: Women and Song*

Black women have been engaged in a struggle for liberation and self-determination in the United States and the West Indies ever since they were wrenched from Africa as unwilling slaves. They have long been aware that they must fight not only white discrimination but also the sexist attitudes that have been implanted in the minds of too many black, as well as white, men. Resistance to racist oppression and male chauvinism has recently been reinforced by an awareness that fundamental changes in the position of black women can come about only if the inequalities of the economic system are challenged. While most women feel that it is unlikely that they can effect any immediate or major changes in the economic or political power structure, they can make it clear that they want such changes, and they are demanding an increased amount of control over their own lives and seeking freedom from all types of oppression. In "I AM WOMAN" Betty Wright powerfully affirms the refusal of black women and of all women to be dominated, exploited, or treated as inferior.[1]

A determination to be as independent and autonomous as possible had characterized the behavior of black women from the time they were seized as slaves in Africa and transported to the alien shores of the United States or islands of the West Indies. Some women chose the most extreme form of resistance—escape by suicide: Those who could not bear the idea of enslavement hurled themselves into the sea from the slave ships, while others killed themselves when faced with intolerable conditions in the new world. Most black women clung to life tenaciously and maintained their independence and self-respect by subtle and devious, as well as open and daring, forms of resistance. Their resilience and strength were forged in the furnace of a cruel and inhumane institution, and black women used that resilience and strength to reshape the institution so that it became less barbaric and damaging. Many black women were beaten and raped, but others refused to allow such unacceptable liberties to be taken with their bodies. Historical evidence abounds to support the fact that black women in the United States frequently and successfully refused to be physically abused.[2] Such instances seem less common in the West Indies, but this may be because there were proportionately fewer slave women in the islands.

Black slave women throughout the American South and the Caribbean were feared for their propensity to poison harsh masters or burn their property. As guardians of the family, black mothers often refused to be parted from their children, and always protected a sense of family unity and self-reliance. Women were active in slave rebellions and crucial in the escape network.[3] Some slave songs were specially used by women active in that escape network—Harriet Tubman had "Steal Away" as a code song to call slaves to escape on the Underground Railroad. Slave songs in general were imbued with multiple elements of resistance. The very musical patterns of their spirituals were a symptom of the refusal of black men and women to abandon their African cultural heritage, and the words were frequently rebellious and subversive.[4]

Throughout slavery, songs sung by women rarely differed from those sung by men. Slavery as an institution failed to divide black men and women, and this unity against a harsh system of economic exploitation was reflected in song. As songs that were communally sung, it is likely that the spirituals stressed unity even when some differences may have existed.

In the years after emancipation, blues developed as a more solitary musical form; and by the time blues recordings were first made, there was a large collection of songs dealing essentially with black women's determination not to be oppressed by men. Women continue to sing about racial prejudice and discrimination, and to explore the possibilities of radical solutions in music as in life, but it is more common for them to articulate a very definite sense of independence from unacceptable roles and unacceptable men. Such songs were, of course "safer" and more likely to find their way onto disks than those which clearly attacked white society or the white political system.

This is a problem that many songs by black women solve by being ambivalent in their focus. Some lyrics leave it open to the listener to decide whether freedom or respect from men, or society at large, is being sought.

This ambivalence reflects a dilemma many black women have been familiar with for decades. They have long been aware that in the battle against racism and sexism, they would ideally like to fight both together. Life, however, is rarely ideal or simple, and it has often seemed necessary to accept some degree of chauvinism in order to fight racism alongside black men. A few black women have elected to face the racism endemic in many phases and branches of the women's movement in order to fight sexism. Economic inequality was a less contentious, but also less common, focal point. The contrast between the poverty of most black people and the wealth of the rich exploiter was condemned in several blues songs by black women in the 1920s and 1930s. The most famous is certainly Bessie Smith's "Poor Man Blues," recorded in the late 1920s.[5] By the 1970s Elaine Brown, a stunning singer and songwriter who was also deputy minister of information for the Black Panthers, was convinced that black people should stamp out inequality and "Seize the Time" to bring about fundamental changes in the political and economic system.[6] To Nina Simone, the only way this can be done is through "Revolution" and "Destruction."[7]

There is an explosive dynamism coursing through the songs that black women write specifically about themselves—a tension that springs from the determination to free themselves from male domination and misuse, conflicting with a strong resolution to stand with black men in the fight for the liberation of all black people. Black men are at once enemies and allies, and have been viewed fairly consistently in this way by black women for well over a century. Black women have worked too long for their living, whether it was in the fields, or in domestic service, or in whatever jobs they could find, to view themselves as the helpless dependents that white women have sometimes been. A rather more particular resentment has built up over the fact that black women have the worst pay, and the lowest status and least interesting jobs, in the United States. As Frances Beal pointed out:

Since her arrival on these shores, the black woman has been subjected to the worst kinds of exploitation and oppression. As a black, she has had to endure all the horrors of slavery and living in a racist society; as a worker she has been the object of continual exploitation, occupying the lowest place on the wage scale and restricted to the most demeaning and uncreative jobs. . . . As a revolutionary she will take an active part in changing the reality.[8]

Angela Davis saw such exploitation as being typical of the plight of black women outside as well as within the United States.[9] Judy Mowatt sings of "Black Woman" in a way that centers on the West Indies but could equally well be applied to the United States: She uses the struggles and heavy loads of the past to provide a foundation for freedom in life and in song.[10] Her cry to "free yourself" finds a persistent echo in the songs of other black women. Freedom is the elusive quality that is more consistently sought than any other. Apart from the obvious, intrinsic appeal of freedom itself, it is also an ideal that resolves the persistent dilemma of the black woman. So long as the words are sufficiently vague or ambiguous, she can be seeking freedom from racism, chauvinism, or economic oppression: Nina Simone sings of freedom as a release from chains,[11] Deniece Williams insists that she has got "to be free,"[12] Fontanella Bass is "Talking About Freedom," and Syreeta is seeking "Freedom,"[13] Equally open to a variety of interpretations is Aretha Franklin's "Think" when she demands "freedom."[14]

A much more concrete conception of freedom was the central inspiration of the earliest songs that black American women sang. A passion for freedom from the restraints of slavery was the prime emotion running through the spirituals. The freedom that was so highly sought was the freedom not to be owned or controlled by another person or restricted by laws that demeaned people and reduced them to the level of property. In spirituals like "O Freedom" this yearning is very powerfully projected and very barely masked. Lines like "Before I'd be a slave I'd be buried in my grave" are hardly ambivalent.[15] Women sang selected spirituals to help inculcate and nurture a burning desire for freedom in their children. Several spirituals were used as code songs for escape by women, like Harriet Tubman, who helped black people to escape to the North and freedom. Harriet Tubman is remembered as having used "Steal Away" and "Go Down, Moses" as her most constant clarion calls to freedom. Both songs were singularly appropriate, and "Go Down, Moses" has been called "one of the great freedom declarations of literature and history":

Let my people go!
Oppressed so hard they could not stand,
Let my people go!

No more in bondage shall they toil,
Let my people go![16]

Almost as popular was an escape spiritual that had no trace of ambiguity:

I'm on the way to Canada
  That cold and bleary land
De sad effects of slavery
  I can't no longer stand
I've served my Master all my days
  Without a dime reward,
And now I'm forced to run away,
  To flee de lash, abroad
Farewell, old Master, don't think hard of me,
I'm traveling to Canada, where all the slaves are free.[17]

Disillusionment set in when it was realized that emancipation from slavery did not bring real freedom. Songs of frustration were poured out, but they were often lightened by a boundless optimism, as in "Northbound Blues" by Maggie Jones (Faye Barnes), which was recorded in the early 1920s:

Goin North, chile, where I can be free
Goin North, chile, where I can be free
Where there's no hardship, like in Tennessee.[18]

A similar spirit of hope suffuses Nancy Wilson's timeless and poignant version of "Black Is Beautiful," which ends with the promise of freedom before death.[19] Although Judy Mowatt wants to see oppressive conditions changed, she also believes that black people can free themselves from a mental condition of slavery. Whereas in "Concrete Jungle" she mourns that even though chains have been removed, she is not free, in "Slavery" she celebrates her freedom from "slave mentality."[20] Rita Marley, who sang with Judy Mowatt in the I-Threes, Bob Marley's back-up singers, seems to agree that freedom can come only through changed attitudes and circumstances.[21] To Labelle, on *Pressure Cookin'*, it seems obvious that freedom can come only through the kind of fundamental changes that require a revolution to accomplish—an idea she sings about with wit, intelligence, and passion.[22]

Some black women have consistently interpreted freedom as personal and emotional. Blues singer Koko Taylor's "Be What You Want to Be" is a typically assertive call for individual freedom.[23] Very much in the same mold is Tina Turner's "Bold Soul Sister," which tells women to be whatever they want to be, how and when they want it.[24] Far more subtle but still projecting the same idea of individual autonomy is the classic "Tain't Nobody's Business if I Do"—sung by Bessie Smith or Billie Holiday, it is a statement of individual freedom sought and gained.[25] Thelma Houston's "Midnight Mona" is hardly a song of the same stature, but it does make the point that, whether because of a consciousness of the slave past or not, the modern black woman cannot be owned.[26]

With some recent songs by black women the search for individual freedom tips over into the realms of the self-indulgent. Natalie Cole's "I'm Ready" and Diana Ross's "It's My Turn" seem somewhat overly self-obsessed.[27] Diana Ross thinks she can "be free" only by "living for myself," as "this time's just for me." Not substantially different, yet somehow more realistic and positive, are Brenda Russell's lyrics for Patrice Rushen's "Breakout," which urge freedom from restraints that stop full exercise of female potential.[28]

One of the most intelligent and compelling calls for freedom came from Amazulu in the early 1980s. This British-based reggae band of five women and one man used to summon people to seek freedom at all levels: freedom for women and men, for blacks and whites, freedom from war, and freedom from inequality and oppression. It was a band to be watched and listened to. While songs like Amazulu's "Greenham Time" and "Brixton" are great to dance to, they appeal most strongly to the brain and the heart, and the strength of their complex appeal for freedom cannot lightly be denied.[29]

A corollary of this search for freedom and independence is that men have often been analyzed very critically and been found wanting. It is a mark of the courage of black women that they have often chosen to discard men that they have found unsuitable. They have never lacked the strength to be alone and have always retained the freedom to choose whether to live with someone or by themselves. They have refused to allow their choices to be confined by current societal mores. Perhaps that has been one of the advantages of being outside the mainstream of American, West Indian, and black British society. For most African women the situation has been very different and far more constraining, and it is only recently that they have been able to move toward any position of assertive independence.

One of the more surprising aspects of songs sung by black American women about their own attitudes and responses to men is how little they have changed. Whereas white women made rapid progress toward independence and self-realization in the second half of the twentieth century, black women had always been independent and self-aware, and this was constantly reflected in their music. There are wonderful examples of the assertive independence of black women during the 1920s captured on records. Singers from the famous, like Ma Rainey and Bessie Smith, through the well-known, such as Memphis Minnie and Victoria Spivey, to the relatively unknown Mary Dixon, Gladys Bentley, and Bessie Brown, sang of their lack of dependence on inadequate men and their determination to lead their own lives.

Attitudes that white feminists later developed toward men were clearly articulated by black blues singers in the 1920s and 1930s—from the indiscriminate condemnation of Bessie Brown's "Ain't Much Good in the Best of Men" (1926) to Rosa Henderson, who wanted a "real good pal," not a poseur looking "cute," in "Can't Be Bothered with No Sheik" (1931). She is not prepared to accept a "substitute" for a "real man"—that would not be worth either the time or the trouble involved.[30]

Rosa Henderson also had a successful 1920s single that made it clear "If you don't give me what I want," she'd find someone who would.[31] A "take it or leave it" attitude to men was common among women blues singers of the era. It was wonderfully illustrated by Bessie Smith's cynical recording of "If You Don't, I Know Who Will."[32] Edith Wilson went further and spat out "I Don't Want Nobody," while Lucille Bogan claimed that "Women Don't Need No Men." Lucille Hegamin made the original record of "Hard-Hearted Hannah" and proved that a woman could be as tough, brutal, and unemotional as any man.[33] Some women went further than mistreating their men, they shot them! Ida Cox satirized this extreme reaction to men's ineptitude on "How Can I Miss You When I've Got Dead Aim," and Victoria Spivey mulled over the consequences of "Murder in the First Degree."[34] More common expressions of disapproval were Maggie Jones's "You Ain't Gonna Feed in My Backyard No

More" and Mary Dixon's "You Can't Sleep in My Bed." Blue Lou Barker said it best when she quipped, "I'm too wise for you to jive" and her man was "too dumb to realize," in "I Don't Dig You, Jack."[35]

Classic blues singers were notorious for the way they satirized men, but they were also famous for the honesty of their portrayal. They projected an image of women as strong and indomitable. Ma Rainey, for instance, could "balance misery with humor, sorrow with anger, outer chaos with inner will," and sing of "women who do not fall to pieces when love is gone, of a prostitute who leaves her pimp, of a lesbian who flaunts her preference." In aggressive, assertive blues like "Prove It on Me Blues," "Trust No Man," "Hustlin' Blues," "Black Eye Blues," "Louisiana Hoodoo Blues," and "Rough and Tumble Blues," she celebrated the independence of black women.[36] The mere sound of Bessie Smith's voice bore witness to her independence and assurance, and in blues like "Young Woman's Blues," "I've Got What It Takes," and "Tain't Nobody's Business," she made it clear that nobody could control or manipulate her life.[37] Equally independent, though less well known, was Bernice Edwards, who sang in "Long Tall Mama" that I do "just what I want to do."[38] In a song where Memphis Minnie is reprimanded for mistreating her man, she unrepentantly celebrates the fact that she lives the life she loves, and "I love the life I live."[39]

Billie Holiday, who, more than anyone else, put all she felt and had experienced into her singing, laid down on disk several classic anthems to female independence. The most powerful song she ever wrote was "God Bless the Child," a subtle statement of self-reliance that has often been quoted by black activists and black poets. Her version of "Tain't Nobody's Business" was as implacable as Bessie Smith's, and there is no mistaking the message of "Baby, Get Lost."[40]

Nina Simone has a similar ability to expose emotions that most people are only half aware even exist. Although she was writing "Four Women" in the 1970s, she went back to slavery as an explanation for the toughness of black women who are embittered and resilient because of the enslavement of their ancestors.[41]

In the same decade "women's lib soul" was popularized by singers like Laura Lee with "Wedlock Is a Padlock" and groups such as Labelle. In Britain in the 1970s and early 1980s Joan Armatrading stands legs apart and exults in being as strong and assertive as a man. On "Kissin' and Huggin'," it's she who wants to take her love for a walk; on "Warm Love," it's she who wants to be the Romeo of the relationship, not a "porcelain Juliet."[42] A more humorous kind of role reversal was The Weather Girls' huge 1983 disco success "It's Raining Men"—those girls were out to get "absolutely soaked in men!"[43] A subtle kind of role reversal is apparent even in songs about lovers not leaving. There is no trace of the whimpering plea in either Lorraine Ellison's magnificent and commanding "Stay with Me" or Jennifer Holliday's "And I'm Telling You I'm Not Going."[44]

There is nothing subtle about the role reversal that is usual in most of Millie Jackson's songs. There is, however, an abundance of wit and sharp observation. Songs like "Never Change Your Lovers in the Middle of the Night" spill over with wicked delight in the power that can be exercised by an unconventional woman.[45] She is just the kind of woman that Michelle Wallace seems to be referring to in *Black Macho* when she says that many black men thought "the black women had gotten out of hand. She was too strong, too hard, too evil, too castrating. . . . The black woman should be more submissive and, above all, keep her big black mouth shut."[46]

Black American women had, of course, always been tough and independent, but it was relatively novel to find African women like Letta Mbulu singing songs like "Ain't No Way to Treat a Lady" in 1977.[47] Miatta Fahnbulleh was a determined rebel against the prejudice that operated against African women singing popular music, and in 1978 she incorporated some of that obstinate rebellion into a song called "Ain't No Way for a Woman,"[48] A similar spirit of rebellious independence, but here linked significantly to a sense of power, slides through Jamaican-born, American-bred Grace Jones's *Nipple to the Bottle* as she sings that she will neither give in nor feel guilty.[49] A different kind of independence and a sensual kind of warning are poured out by Anita Baker, the soul sensation of the mid-1980s. With her beautiful, resonant voice that can dip to unknown depths she warns her men to "Watch Your Step." She is not a woman about to be walked over (*Sweet Love/Watch Your Step*, Electra EKR 44T, 1986).

It is another symptom of female independence, tipping over into a kind of role reversal, that many black American women like Grace Jones, Donna Summer, and Millie Jackson sing songs that are sexually explicit. One writer on soul music has claimed that this is a fairly recent phenomenon,[50] but if you listen to women's blues of the 1920s and 1930s, there will be no doubt it is a well-established tradition. Bessie Smith's "Nobody in Town Can Bake a Sweet Jelly Roll like

Mine" and "Kitchen Man" confused no one with their obvious innuendo.[51] Rather more crude but enormously popular was Susie
Edwards's rendition of "I Want a Hot Dog for My Roll."[52] Far more
sophisticated in its rich, disturbing sexuality was Victoria Spivey's
allegorical "Black Snake Blues." Spivey also provided what was no
more than a thinly disguised description of sexual intercourse in
"Organ Grinder Blues".[53]

Even the thinnest of allusory veils were discarded on endless blues
like "Do It a Long Time, Papa" by Faye Barnes[54] or "One Hour
Mama" by Ida Cox, who made it clear that she had no time for a "one-
minute pappa" or any man who could not prove he had
"endurance."[55] It's surprising how close these words are to those of
Millie Jackson's "All the Way, Lover," written fifty years later. She
demands similar endurance to get fulfillment because "frustration
ain't no fun."[56] Millie Jackson sensuously adds the moans suggestive
of ongoing sex that Donna Summer also made part of soul music's
repertoire. Very much her own, though, is Jackson's sexual "rap."
Into "If Loving You Is Wrong, I Don't Want to Be Right," on the
brilliant album *Caught Up*, she interjects a rap about an affair with a
married man having the advantage that you "get your piece" two or
three times a week, whereas a wife is lucky if she gets it once![57] Shirley
Brown is another soul lady who has become increasingly straightforward in her sexual allusions. In "Long on Lovin'" she comments, "It
ain't the size of the ship, it's the motion of the ocean."[58] Denise
Lasalle is even more explicit about the inadequacies of her love, who
"left his job half-done" and whose place is now more satisfactorily
filled by a younger man. She is equally unrestrained on tracks like
"Come to Bed," "Down Home Blues (Rated X)," "Lay Me Down,"
and "This Bell Was Made for Ringing."[59] Laura Lee is another black
American woman who consistently sings powerful songs of liberation, defiance, and lust. She is at her most torrid on "I Need It Just as
Bad as You."[60] Such honesty is a mark of the way black women feel
they can project what they are in music, regardless of the embarrass-
ment they may cause or the illusions they shatter.

Honesty has always been one of the most obvious characteristics of
the way black women project themselves in song. Another of the
dominant qualities to come across in their music is resilience. Just as
Jamaican Judy Mowatt celebrates that resilience in "Black Woman" and
"Strength to Go Through," Marcia Griffiths (who was with Judy
Mowatt in the I-Threes) sings spiritedly of "Survival."[61] It is quality that

was woven into the very fabric of the lives and songs of women like Bessie Smith, whose spirit was indomitable whatever the trouble she faced. Bessie Smith was sure in "Long Old Road" that she would reach her goal in the end, however many hardships she met on the way.[62]

More recently songs by Etta James, Koko Taylor, Nina Simone, Minnie Riperton, Gladys Knight, Thelma Houston, Donna Summer, Irma Thomas, Betty Everett, Ann Peebles, Tina Turner, Natalie Cole, and Millie Jackson have explored every aspect of black women's special, hardship-honed ability to cope with the blows dealt out by life and love, and to bounce back *smiling*. Diana Ross turns defeat to defiance in "I Ain't Been Licked;"[63] and to a disco beat, Gloria Gaynor pounds out the most successful celebration of the survival impulse when she sings "I Will Survive."[64]

There are obviously black women who have suffered, and sing not of survival but of defeat and failure. There are also a great many black women who sing mainly of love in all its aspects, true and false, lasting and transitory, romantic and deep. But the surprising thing is that so many black women sing with honesty and passion about what they want and what they are. Even those who might not go so far as to demand freedom would certainly join with Aretha Franklin in seeking "Respect."[65] Franklin's dramatic 1967 interpretation of Otis Redding's "Respect" seemed to insist that respect be given to each black woman and to all black people. The delivery of the song was as important as the words, and Franklin's version became no less than an anthem for a turbulent period of struggle for black rights. More recently (1983) and very much more personally, Lydia Murdoch's "Superstar" has asked for that very same thing—"respect": "Superstar" was written as a specific response to "Billie Jean," a song by Michael Jackson that denied paternity. It is a deliberate attempt to project a woman's point of view, and that woman is depicted as independent and self-sustaining, determined that the world will know the truth. She will not be appeased until she gets that respect, because she is "mad as hell."[66]

Black women are still discriminated against and exploited, both individually and as a group. They still have a great deal to fight for on personal, social, economic, and political levels, and they are committed to continuing to fight. As Aretha Franklin put it, "Ain't Nobody Gonna Turn Me Around."[67] Their pride in themselves and their resolution that they will win equally on all levels shine through their music. Their independence and autonomy, their individuality and their spirit, were captured by a disco hit in the United States during the autumn of 1983, sung by Gloria Gaynor. Its title summed up women's determination to be themselves: "I Am What I Am."[68]

Sweet Honey in the Rock also sings assertive, independent songs. "Ella's Song" (*Listen to the Rhythm*, SPIN 106), written by lead singer Bernice Reagon, ends with the positive statement that she will bow to no man's word. In 1986 Jaki Graham—black, British, and full of optimism and vitality—sang with consummate energy and multiple meanings, "Set Me Free." A cry from and for all women of the 1980s.

NOTES

1. Betty Wright, "I AM WOMAN," *I AM WOMAN*, Polystar WOMTV1 (1973).

2. Thomas Webber, *Deep Like the Rivers* (New York: Norton, 1978), p. 166; Gerda Lerner, *Black Women in White America: A Documentary History* (New York: Random House, 1972), pp. 24–25, 35; Frederick Douglass, *The Life and Times of Frederick Douglass* (New York: Collier, 1962), p. 52.

3. Mary Ellison, "Resistance to Oppression: Black Women's Response to Slavery," *Slavery and Abolition*, Spring 1984, pp. 56–63.

4. Dena Epstein, *Sinful Tunes and Spirituals: Black Folk Music to the Civil War* (Urbana: University of Illinois Press, 1977), pp. 77–89, 125–137, 363–365, 373–374.

5. Bessie Smith, *Empty Bed Blues*, Columbia 66273.

6. Elaine Brown, *Seize the Time*, Vault 131 (1970).

7. Nina Simone, *Take off Black Soul*, RCA CL42220.

8. Francis M. Beal, "Slave of a Slave No More: Black Women in Struggle," *Black Scholar*, March 1975, pp. 2, 10.

9. Angela Davis, *Women, Race and Class* (Shoreditch: Women's Press, 1981), pp. 200–201, 244, and *If They Come in the Morning* (London: Corbach and Chambers, 1971), p. 188.

10. Judy Mowatt, *Black Woman*, Island/Grove ILPS 9649.

11. Nina Simone, *The Best of Nina Simone*, RCA Victor LSP 4374.

12. Deniece Williams, "Free," *I AM WOMAN*, Polystar WOMTV1.

13. Fontanella Bass, *Talking About Freedom*, Contempo 02032 45; Syreeta, "Freedom," *The Spell*, Tamla T7 349.

14. Aretha Franklin, *Aretha's Gold*, Atlantic SD 8227.

15. John Lovell, Jr., *Black Songs: The Forge and the Flame* (New York: Macmillan, 1972), pp. 386–387.

16. Lovell, *Black Song*, pp. 326–327.

17. Sarah Bradford, *Harriet Tubman, the Moses of Her People* (New York: Corinth, 1961), p. 49.

18. Quoted in Derrick Stewart-Baxter, ed., *Ma Rainey and the Classic Blues Singers* (London: Studio Vista, 1970), p. 76.

19. Nancy Wilson, "Black Is Beautiful," *The Sound of Nancy Wilson*, Capital S2970.

20. Judy Mowatt, *Black Woman*.

21. Malu Halasa, "Jamaican Nightmare," *Black Music and Jazz Review*, January 1983, pp. 2–3; Rita Marley, *Who Feels It Knows It*, Island 9803.

22. Labelle, *Pressure Cookin'*, RCA 3307 (1974); Tony Cummings, "Labelle: I Sold My Heart to the Rock Man," *Black Music*, April 1974, pp. 20–22.

23. Koko Taylor, "Be What You Want to Be," *I Got What It Takes*, Sonet SNJF 687.

24. Tina Turner, "Bold Soul Sister," *The Hunter*, GMP SHSP.

25. Bessie Smith, "Tain't Nobody's Business if I Do," *The World's Greatest Blues Singer*, CBS 66258.

26. Thelma Houston, "Midnight Mona," *Ready to Roll*, Tamla J736IRI (1978).

27. Natalie Cole, *I'm Ready*, Epic EPC 25P39 (1983); Diana Ross, *It's My Turn*, Motown TMG 1217–45 (1980).

28. Patrice Rushen, "Breakout," *Straight from the Heart*, K52352 (1983).

29. Amazulu Live at City of London Polytechnic, October 1983, and University of Keele, October 13, 1983. Amazulu, "Greenham Time" (B side of *Cairo*), Towerbell 12 TWO 35B45, and "Brixton" (B side of *Smylee Stylee*), Towerbell 45.

30. *Mean Mothers: Independent Women's Blues*, Vol. I, Rosetta Records RR1 300.

31. Stewart-Baxter, *Ma Rainey*, p. 34.

32. Bessie Smith, *The World's Greatest Blues Singer*, CBS 66258.

33. Stewart-Baxter, *Ma Rainey*, pp. 28, 24; Lucille Bogan, *Women Don't Need No Men*, Agram 2005.

34. Ida Cox, *Blues Ain't Nothing Else but Milestones*, MFP 2015; Victoria Spivey, *The Recorded Legacy of the Blues*, Spivey Reissues LP 2001.

35. *Mean Mothers*.

36. Sarah Lieb, *Mother of the Blues. A Study of Ma Rainey* (Boston: University of Massachusetts Press, 1981), pp. 171–172.

37. Bessie Smith, *Nobody's Blues but Mine*, Columbia G31093; *Any Woman's Blues*, Columbia G30126; *The World's Greatest Blues singer*, CBS 66258.

38. *Mean Mothers*.

39. Memphis Minnie, "Hold Me Blues," *Memphis Minnie 1941–1949*, Flyright LP 109.

40. Billie Holiday, *God Bless the Child*, CBS M66267; *Mean Mothers*; Hettie Jones, *Big Star, Fallin' Mama. Five Women in Black Music* (New York: Viking Press, 1974), p. 90.

41. Nina Simone, *Wild Is the Wind*, Philips PHS 600 207.

42. Chris May, "Joan Armatrading," *Black Music*, January 1977, 1978, pp. 8–12; Joan Armatrading, *Show Some Emotion*, A&M AMLH 68433, *To the Limit*, A&M AMLH 64732, *Walk Under Ladders*, A&M AMLH 64876, and *The Key*, A&M AMLX 64912.

43. The Weather Girls, *It's Raining Men*, CBS A13-292445 (1982).

44. Lorraine Ellison, *Stay with Me*, WB Tro Music 45K16001; Jennifer Holliday, *And I'm Telling You I'm not Going*, CBS Geffen GEF A2644.

45. Millie Jackson, *A Moment's Pleasure*, Spring SP16722.

46. Michelle Wallace, *Black Macho and the Myth of Superman* (London: John Calder, 1979), p. 11.

47. "Afro-Heat," *Black Music*, April 1977, p. 51.

48. "Afro-Heat," *Black Music*, January 1978, p. 50.

49. Grace Jones, *Nipple to the Bottle*, Island WIP 6779 45.

50. Ian Hoare, "Mighty, Mighty Spade and Whitey: Soul Lyrics and Black-White Crosscurrents," in Ian Hoare, Clive Anderson, Tony Cummings, and Simon Frith, *The Soul Book* (London: Methuen, 1975), pp. 136–145.

51. Bessie Smith, *The World's Greatest Blues Singer*, CBS 66258.

52. Butterbeans and Susie, "I Want a Hot Dog for My Roll," *Stars of the Apollo Theatre*, CBS 67203.

53. Spivey, *Recorded Legacy*.

54. Faye Barnes, *Do It a Long Time, Papa*, Black Swan 12136.

55. *Mean Mothers*.

56. Millie Jackson, *Feelin' Bitchy*, Spring/Polydor Super 2391 301 (1977).

57. John Morthland, "Millie Jackson: Gettin' Her Piece," pp. 9–10. *Black Music*, November 1975; Millie Jackson, *Caught Up*, Polydor 3902 (1975).

58. Shirley Brown, *Shirley Brown*, Arista Sparty 1017.

59. Denise Lasalle, *The Bitch Is Bad*, ABC 1027, *Here I Am Again*, WEA 1p 209; *Second Breath*, ABC D-966.

60. Laura Lee, *I Can't Make It Alone*, Inv KZ 33133.

61. Mowatt, *Black Woman*; Marcia Griffiths, *Naturally*, High Note DP 1003 (1977).

62. Smith, *World's Greatest Blues Singer*, CBS 66258.

63. Diana Ross, *The Boss*, Motown M7-923 RI.

64. Gloria Gaynor, *I Will Survive*, Polydor 2095 017 45.

65. Aretha Franklin, *Aretha's Greatest Hits*, Atlantic 2400 188.

66. Lydia Murdoch, *Superstar*, Korova KOW 30/T 45; "Talk, Talk," *Melody Maker*, October 29, 1983; "She's Billie Jean and She's Mad as Hell," *Black Echoes*, October 29, 1983.

67. Aretha Franklin, *2 Originals of Aretha Franklin*, Atlantic K80007.

68. Gloria Gaynor, *I Am What I Am*, Silver Blue, 73.

6   *Used and Abused? A Male Perspective*

Men are not usually seen as an oppressed group because they are thought to be dominant in almost every sphere of life. Yet this is obviously less true of black men. They have been treated as inferior not only in the United States, the Caribbean, and Britain but also in many of the English-speaking African nations. White dominance has pushed them into positions of such ignominy and subservience that their pride and masculinity have been threatened. Sometimes the aggression to which they have been subjected has been turned onto women; on occasion, it has been internalized and has crippled their ability to relate openly to women or indeed, to anyone.

Yet frequently it is women themselves who provoke the anger and resentment of men. Woman have similarly used men as a release for all the frustration they feel about their own predicament. Some are even aware of the irony that without female collusion, women could never have been relegated to the bedroom and the kitchen. Some men are aware of this and feel an indignation that is often expressed in song. Others sorrowfully attack the women who unthinkingly burden their men of today with the collective guilt of generations.

Men in the 1980s, in song as well as in life, display symptoms of confusion. What do women want or expect of them? Should they— can they—treat women as complete equals? Or do women really want some element of male dominance? Should they be "sensitive" or "macho," "understanding" or decisive? Songs don't come up with definitive answers, but they articulate very clearly a wide range of problems, fears, resentments, and assertions. One of the greatest fears is the very common human fear of rejection. When a woman leaves a man (or vice versa), anger, as well as a sense of loss, is experienced by the one left behind.

National boundaries are not important in affairs of the heart, even though national attitudes to women vary greatly from country to country. Almost every country has men who mistreat their women and wonder why they are abandoned, just as every nation has men who are trying to combat chauvinistic impulses and to do their utmost to treat women well, or even as equals. Not surprisingly, they are the most surprised and the most hurt when they, too, are cheated on, manipulated, or left.

Men, far more than women, have to cope with being abandonded. It has become a statistical fact that in the West women tend to be the ones who leave or break up a marriage or a relationship. Certainly in the United States and Britain, most divorces are initiated by women. This may change as women feel capable of asking for more of their needs to be met by the men they love. Up to now, most have done what they can to make a relationship work without subsuming too many of their own wants and aspirations, but have found it preferable to get out rather than get too demanding. Often there is a well-based feeling that those demands will not be met, and if hope and prayer haven't produced change, the optimism may survive but transfer itself to a new relationship. This obviously means that some men feel not only rejected but also bewildered. The less sensitive will compound this with indignation and self-justification. The more aware ask why. What can be done? Some of them ask it in song. Others shift between anger and self-hatred at their inability to change. They mourn it in song.

It is possible that men need song as an expression of their more vulnerable and sensitive selves at least as much as women do. It is far less socially acceptable for men to appear either vulnerable or sensitive. Yet all men are vulnerable and sensitive to a greater or lesser degree. Singers can be more open about the fact that they can be, and are, hurt, and they can help to explain and ease the pain felt by so many. Songs about inadequacy and loss, failure and despair, can be cathartic, and they can lead the men who listen to begin to acknowledge their own needs and inadequacies.

In "Kind-Hearted Woman Blues," Robert Johnson attacks "evil-hearted women," who will not let him be. In his classic, anguished "Love in Vain," he seems inconsolable over the loss of a girlfriend and despairingly mourns: "All my love's in vain." In another song he complains about being exploited by his woman: "She's got a mortgage on my body, a lien on my soul."[1]

Elmore James is typical of the hundreds of male blues singers who feel wronged by their women. His "Sinful Woman" is one of those women who seem to beset blues singers. She is mean and unfaithful, and drives her man out of his mind. In "I Was a Fool" he curses himself for believing his lying woman, and is tough enough to tell her goodbye. He gives his woman another chance to behave in a loving way in "Baby, What's Wrong," but he still chastizes her for not treating him right. His most famous number, "The Sky Is Crying," embodies all the hurt and rejection of knowing that someone you love has stopped caring. It is the ultimate pain-wracked denunciation of the fickleness of some females. In "Late Hours at Midnight," James asks why his woman can't treat him right, and denounces her "evil ways" that "won't let me sleep at night." He determines to find another woman who will "treat him right." Yet he is left with the pain of knowing he will love her wherever he goes.[2]

Muddy Waters is among the numerous bluesmen who had cause to ask agrievedly, "Where's My Woman Been" (*Rare and Unissued*, Green Line GCH 8010). Otis Rush is representative of a perspective on unfaithful women that is only slightly different when he sings "Will My Woman Be Home Tonight" (*So Many Roads Live, in Concert*, Delmark DS 643). Big Bill Broonzy goes further and condemns a "Bad Acting Woman," and in the title of another song on the same album sings out, "Stop Lying, Woman" (*Midnight Steppers*, Bluetime, BT2001).

Tampa Red has the "Grievin' and Worryin' Blues" (*Tampa Red*, Vol. I, Bluebird No. 11, RCA PM 42029, 1984) because his baby doesn't treat him right. He tries to turn the tables by warning that if she leaves him and decides to come back, she may find him loving someone else. Tampa Red's real name was Hudson Whittaker, which somehow feels more in keeping with the sad and solemn songs he sings about his unfaithful, too frequently departing women.

Atlanta bluesman Curly Weaver is equally condemnatory of the woman who "Don't Treat Me No Good No More," and Blind Willie McTell was just as disillusioned by female perfidy in the 1930s when he recorded "Married Life's a Pain."[3]

More complex are some of the songs that come from West Coast bluesmen like T-Bone Walker and Charles Brown. T-Bone Walker wrote and sang a convoluted saga of loving an unloving woman in "I Got the Blues Again." In "You Don't Love Me" he seems so numbed by the way he is being mistreated that he stops caring about his woman, himself, or the relationship. Equally destructive is the way Charles Brown, a Los Angeles pianist and vocalist, is abused by the woman he loves. He begs her to take him back, as he feels his self-respect slipping away. Without her he feels that he has nobody to care for him and that he will become innately worthless.[4]

One of the most chilling male indictments of woman and relationships comes from bluesmen as varied as T-Bone Walker, Albert Collins, Phil Guy, and Robert Cray singing "Cold, Cold Feeling." They know a relationship must end when they start to feel "ice around my heart," and recognize they are being treated like prisoners and fools.[5] Albert Collins, on another occasion, sings "A Good Fool Is Hard to Find." Before a simmering solo from his supposedly icy guitar, he accuses his woman of being cold and unfeeling, manipulative and devious. Albert Collins may come over as nobody's fool, but he obviously feels duped and exploited. In the next track on the same album (*Cold Snap*, Alligator/Sonet SNTF 969, 1986), "Lights Are on but Nobody's Home," he is convinced his wife is a lying cheat and is unfairly playing with his mind. Albert Collins plays a guitar that ranges from wild and jangling to a contained, restrained anger. His lyrics are intelligent and perceptive—he asks his woman how he can love her if the love she gives, she keeps on "snatching back." He knows she loves him but is too frightened of rejection to be totally committed. He realizes that another man must have loved her and then "left her behind," and he assures her that he will not hurt her or do anything she does not want.

Bobby Bland had one of the most desolate voices ever to be captured on vinyl; that desolation was often accompanied by anger, and always caused by a woman. His soul-stirring blues—ballads like "Lead Me On" (*Two Steps from the Blues*, Duke X-74)—were cries of anguish with few parallels in blues or soul.

For such a sweet and gentle man, B. B. King's chauvinistic attitude on some of his records and in some live performances comes as an unpleasant surprise. Yet he is drawing on a pool of once acceptable male attitudes when he sings "Don't Answer the Door" and directs his woman not to let in anyone but him. Even her sister is not allowed access, as long as he is paying the bills. Like many bluesmen, he

seems to be rejecting any notion of female independence or autonomy, and like them he is surprised when he is left alone with his
arrogance.[6]

Very different is Robert Cray, who may be the most masculine and
unwimplike of singers, but he still exemplifies the most complete
male/female role reversal in the blues today. In his songs, more
consistently than in those of any other bluesman, it is the man, not the
woman, who is mistreated. His woman confuses him by not wanting
to marry him but still being there to love and care for him. Other
women put him down and use him, and he attempts to work up the
courage to leave them. In "Bad Influence" he claims his woman
"used me" and was always a "bad influence" making him do things he
didn't want and hurting him in "all the worst kinds of ways." In
"Change of Heart, Change of Mind—Same Old Funky Thing," on his
False Accusations album, he mourns the difficulty in finding true
love—his present woman has another man. On the same album he
sings a number called "It's the Last Time I'll be Burned Like This"
and vows never to be a victim of a misusing, abusing lover again. In
"False Accusations" he acts out the "other man" role and is far more
riddled with guilt than Millie Jackson ever was as the other woman.
These are brave songs, for Robert Cray is admitting a human vulnerability, a need for real, unromanticized love that many men would
be reluctant to acknowledge.

No one has described the archetypal black "macho" man better
than the very masculine blues/soul/jazz singer Gil Scott-Heron. He
draws a picture of a superficially romantic, joy-killing egoist who is "a
legend in his own mind and God's gift to women on a day God wasn't
giving up a thing."[7] A woman might have said it as well, but certainly
not better.

James Brown has for years epitomized the "macho" image in
music. His "It's a Man's, Man's, Man's World" (*Soul Classics*, Vol. I,
Poly 5401) does end by saying that the world may belong to men, but
they still need a woman in it; but that only gives women their place at
the cost of putting them firmly in it. James Brown is surprising on
many counts. Contrary to rumor he is the one major R&B artist to
come from South Carolina (Barnwell). He moved to Georgia when
he was four, but his South Carolinian birth is somehow indicative of
his unique qualities. As Charlie Gillet pointed out, " 'Funk' had been
used as one of those euphemistic black expressions for years: it

suggested the smells of sex, a simple lifestyle, and a particular kind of raunchy rhythm which mimicked the grind of love-makers."

New Orleans pianists had played with the beat in a funky way, and bass players such as Larry Graham in Sly Stone's Family Stone introduced the bass "funk" slap. But it was James Brown who "pursued" the idea of funk with the most fanatical dedication. His "Sex Machine" is the archetypal funk glorification of the superstud image. Yet his "Pioneer of Love" shows that he, too, has a vulnerable, easily damaged side that could be exposed by a certain kind of woman.

In soul songs men are also aware of their weakness. Percy Sledge acknowledges that "When a man loves a woman, he can see no wrong." This "deep soul" classic, "When a Man Loves a Woman" (*Any Day Now*, Charly R&B CRB 1078), may have been made on a small budget in a small Alabama studio, but its emotional impact is huge. It is a mournful elegy for all those reationships where the man is the one who is too trusting and is the last to know that his woman is two-timing him. This misplaced trust may cost a man his friends and his integrity, but it is the cost he pays for loving too much. Yet the song also suggests that sometimes it can pay off and his woman, once unworthy, can live up to his trust and expectations. In "It Tears Me Up" (on the same album) Percy Sledge is left in no doubt that he loves a woman who doesn't deserve him. She has cheated on him with his best friend, but he still cannot extricate himself from this paralyzing love.

Isaac Hayes is also representative of those men who trust their women, are blind to their faults, and find they are being cheated on. His "rap" that precedes "By the Time I Get to Phoenix" says more eloquently and specifically what so many men have felt and so many other songs allude to rather than fully explain. The song itself, with its impassioned, sorrowful vocal, explains, against a soulful piano, horn, and percussion, just why he had to leave. He is like the abused wives who forgive their husbands' infidelity until the day they have had enough and have to leave. After seven infidelities Hayes stands for all those husbands who also have had enough and have to leave. That he does it with understanding and the pain of love lost still in his heart makes this record a magnificent account of human turmoil over unfaithfulness and parting.

Harold Melvin, sustained by The Blue Notes, complains in "Hostage" that he is a hostage to the love of the woman who makes him unhappy. Obviously his inability to break away makes him even more unhappy. He wants to be free but cannot extricate himself.[8] Smokey Robinson arguably has written and sung some of the most affecting numbers about heartbreak and the loneliness of desertion. His "Tracks of My Tears" is a luminous classic. His fragile voice is overloaded with pain, and the strong melody carries some of the weight of the misery.[9]

Stevie Wonder is legitimately angry when his woman is unfaithful and clearly says, "I Ain't Gonna Stand for It" (*Hotter than July*, Motown 2C070–64121, 1980). He senses the truths of all the accusations leveled at her and threatens violent retaliation. He similarly laments the untrustworthiness and unfaithfulness of his lover in "Lately." He also is distraught when his woman finds another man in "Tuesday Heartbreak" (*Talking Book*, Tamla-Motown 5C184–50371–72). But the catchy tune and David Sanborn's saxophone give the impression that the "heartbreak" can easily be patched up. His "Ordinary Pain" (*Songs in the Key of Life*, Tamla Motown TMSP 6002) seems a much more serious affair. This is a saga of masochism and regret, of feelings being numbed as nerves are slashed with knives; the voice and music hover uneasily between menace and despair.

Luther Vandross has a velvet voice that wraps itself around defecting women and surrounds them with an aura of sensuality that could well be fatal. On "Until You Come Back to Me" (*Busy Body*, Epic EPC 25608, 1983), the ache of wanting echoes in the nuances of the silkily questing voice and reverberates through the elegant music, superbly produced by Marcus Miller. Few woman could stay away from the voice and the music for long.

In a different style, the superb reggae singer, Dennis Brown questions as well as protests, "Why, Baby Why," when a relationship has fallen apart. His soulful voice turns this reggae lament into a saga that is so sensuous it borders on seduction.[10]

Reggae star Erroll Dunkley is unambivalently "Left with a Broken Heart" (*Special Request*, Carousel CAR LP01, 1982), but the tough delivery and the hard-rocking guitar backing interact with the steady bass and drums to create such a feeling of strength that recovery seems inevitable. The same words may be used by a group of representatives of yet another response. The Paragons are among the reggae groups or individuals that protest with unequivocal desperation about being "Left with a Broken Heart" (*The Paragons Return*, Third World TDWD25, 1981). But here skillful and individualistic harmonies blend with the solid beat to create the sound of deeply frustrated passion.

Equally despondent is the reaction of soul star Jimmy Ruffin to being abandoned. His vocal on "Farewell Is a Lonely Sound" is gut-wrenchingly agonized, and he admits to the tears a man is not supposed to shed when his woman leave him.[11] But it's Jackie Wilson who sings the saddest of the "men abandoned" songs and has produced some of the most anguished, unrequited love songs. Behind that soaring melismatic voice lie subtle vocal harmonies and the orchestral sound palette of massed strings and a solitary, sad piano. On "Lonely Teardrops," his vocal hits a new intensity of sadness and pain, and the music shreds the already torn emotions.[12]

On all these records there is an acute awareness that men are rejected as often as women, and they demonstrate in song a particular anger when they feel a breakup is unnecessary and unjustified. Typical is The Detroit Spinners' "You're Throwing a Good Love Away." The woman who walked away is accused of treating love as a game and knowingly breaking hearts. She is warned that one of these days she will need the love she has so wantonly wasted. The tone of the voice is wry and premonitory rather than hysterical, and this is underlined by the dance beat that builds up to a hypnotic climax as the drums and synthesizer increase the tempo.[13]

When Curtis Mayfield sings a moving lament to the woman who left him, it has a different feel than most others, since he was brought up to believe that women are equal. In "Now You're Gone" (*Roots*, Buddah Super 2318–045) he sings succinctly of his woman's planned desertion and of his own bitter sorrow. The pain is worse because the other man was his friend and brother, and because he didn't realize how much he loved his woman until she was gone. The sadness seems intensified because Mayfield is so self-evidently the most unchauvinistic of men, a man who treats women with respect and as equals. He is a victim of the breakdown that can happen in most relationships, but he seems to deserve this misery far less than most people.

Arguably, Otis Redding seemed just as undeserving, especially since this most soulful of singers had his biggest hit posthumously with "Dock of the Bay." Here he laments a lost love in a voice that is filled with disturbing melancholy. The introspective mood is put into stark perspective by the sinewy, uncluttered guitar played in masterly fashion by Steve Cropper.[14]

Otis Redding also wrote the song that has been used by men and women to demand a basic human right. "Respect" (*Otis Blue*, Atlantic K40003) makes it clear that this had to be the basis for any effective contact between people. The words are emphasized by urgently repeating bass figures from Duck Dunn. The slow dipping vocals on "I've Been Loving You Too Long" (on the same album) are the saddest lament for what people can do to each other if there is not enough real love and respect on both sides.

The Commodores address a similar question when they question the "strong men" stereotype and suggest that people in a relationship concentrate on saying to each other "Let's Do It Right" (Commodores, *Caught in the Act*, Tamla Motown STML 11286). But this does not mean that The Commodores are not as aggrieved as they are when aware a woman is cheating. "You Don't Know That I Know" is a funky rap on unfaithfulness (on the same album).

Other singers and other bands protest for far more vague or more singularly specific reasons. Hip hop and go go seem prone to songs that put women down—often without apparent cause. Typical is the danceable but lyrically vacuous "Girls Ain't Nothin' but Trouble" (Champion Champ 17, 1986). Even a Sugarhill record sleeve decribes Trouble Funk as "ludricrously macho" on "Hey Fellas" (*Rapped Uptight*, Sugarhill SHLD 1001, 1981).

Among the more particular causes for complaint is The Temptations' frustration that while they can "conquer the world" and do impossible things, like living forever, they can't win the love of a desired woman in "I Can't Get Next to You" (*Temptations' Greatest Hits*, Vol. II, Gor G7–954). Even more individual is Michael Jackson's biggest hit. His 1983 *Billboard* no. 1, "Billie Jean," is one long complaint. But it is a new and brilliantly conceived kind of protest. The whinging is offset by the compulsive disco beat and the stunning arrangement, but the lyrics are all directed at establishing that he is not the father of Billie Jean's child. That would, he rages, have been a biological impossibility, since he denies that Billie Jean was his lover. Unjustifiable rumor and unfounded gossip are the real causes of his protest.[15]

The ultimate male indictment of women in song comes from Marvin Gaye. *Here, My Dear* is a solid stretch of uncontrolled sorrow and directed pain. It publicly mourned the death of his marriage to Anna Gordy and censured the fickleness and unreliability of the female species. There is a certain irony in this song that leaps out from the responses of an archetypal male chauvinist who has lost few opportunities to sleep around. Yet this in no way detracts from the power of this song to impart all the pain and anger, all the sense of disillusion and sadness that clearly suffused Gaye at the end of his marriage. This is a cathartic album—one that lives out the experience on vinyl with no concessions to the market, no concessions to anything but the reality of how he feels. This is an album filled with passionate, doleful anger.[16]

A far more conciliatory treatment of a similar theme is laid down on vinyl by Sunny Ade. His *My Dear* single has its critical, dissatisfied aspects, but it is basically part of a constructive attempt to patch up a quarrel with his wife. Since they are apparently reunited, this seems to be functional music at its most effective.

Occasionally men complain about other men's attitudes to women. Trinidad Bill is among the few who protest male exploitation of the female sex. In "Free up the Women" (*Hardness Is Badness*, Charlie's, 1982), Trinidad Bill attacks men who "never stop and think," and he finds the fact that some of them act like pimps even more reprehensible. The attack is delivered over such cheerful music that it seems likley to evoke a positive, rather than a dismissive, response.

One of the most innovative talents of the 1980s is renowned for the freshness and brilliance of his musical ideas and performance, but is almost as well known for his sexuality and penchant for exotic makeup. Yet there is no real gender bending here. Prince may be small and wear eye liner, but he is undeniably erotic in a masculine way and remarkably free from sexist attitudes or preconceptions. His songs more often complain about the damage people do to each other rather than placing blame at the door of a woman. Prince is an odd mixture of apparent superstar or superstud domination and vulnerability and "feminine" images. He may project male sexuality, but he also treats women musicians as complete equals and uses them in his band with style and impact. In "When Doves Cry" he not only uses unusual analogies but also regrets disagreement as much as he protests it. His way of mourning the end of a relationship is complex and different in "Purple Rain."[17] This is a man who catalyzes rethinking as easily as he gets people out on the dance floor.

In some ways, songs are preceding daily behavioral changes. More men emerge as sensitive and vulnerable, as seekers of real equality between men and women, on record than in life. It is possible that songs actually voice emerging attitudes that have yet to find full expression in other ways. Maybe songs can gently push men in the direction of neither exploiting women nor allowing themselves to be exploited. Perhaps songs can even help men relate to women as equals, loving them for what they are and not for what they represent.

NOTES

1. Robert Johnson, *King of the Delta Blues Singers*, CBS 624561.
2. Elmore James, *The Collection: 20 Blues Greats*, Deja Vu DVLP 2035.
3. Bruce Bastin, *Red River Blues: The Blues Tradition in the Southeast* (Basingstoke: Macmillan, 1986), p. 135.
4. *T-Bone Walker Sings the Blues*, Liberty LBY 3047 (1959); Charlie Gillett, *The Sound of the City: The Rise of Rock and Roll*, London: Souvenir Press, 1983.
5. *T-Bone Walker Sings the Blues*; Albert Collins, *Ice Pickin'*, Alligator/Sonet SNTF 707 (1978); Phil Guy, *Bad Luck Boy*, JSP 1061 (1983).
6. B. B. King, *Completely Live and Well*, Charly DX14.
7. Gil Scott-Heron, "A Legend in His Own Mind," *Real Eyes*, Arista AL 9540 (1980).
8. Harold Melvin and The Blue Notes, *Reaching for the World*, ABC/Million Dollar Records AB969 (1976).
9. Smokey Robinson, *Greatest Hits*, Vol. II, Tamla TAM 280.
10. Dennis Brown, *Love Has Found Its Way*, A&M AMCH 64886 (1982).
11. *Motown Hits of Gold*, Vol. V, Motown WL72404.
12. Jackie Wilson, "Please Tell Me Why" and "You Don't Know What It Means," *The Classic Jackie Wilson*, Skratch Music Productions JAK 101.
13. Detroit Spinners, *Yesterday, Today and Tomorrow*, Atlantic SD19100 (1977).
14. *The Best of Otis Redding*, ATCO 2–801.
15. Michael Jackson, *Thriller*, Epic EPC 85930.
16. Marvin Gaye, *Here, My Dear*, Tamla Motown, T364CP2 (1978).
17. Prince and The Revolution, *Purple Rain*, Warner 9251104.

"War: It's Nothing but a Heartbreak": Attitudes to War in Black Lyrics

War! What is it good for?
Absolutely nothing![1]

These strong words were written by Norman Whitfield and Barrat Strong. As sung by Edwin Starr in 1970, they stayed at no. 1 in the *Billboard* charts for three weeks. In the same year, The Temptations recorded the song, and 14 years later it was to reach a new generation through Frankie Goes to Hollywood, as the B side of *Two Tribes*. The antiwar sentiments of the song reflect a recurring black antipathy to any war other than one fought as a revolution for the establishment of justice and liberty. Even then, only a minority has ever felt that was the best way to reach any end, however desirable. The majority of African singers see war as futile and destructive rather than as a means to attain freedom. African songs in English, as well as in native African languages, denounced war as harmful and redundant in the 1970s and 1980s. Nigerian superstar Sonny Okusun sang antiwar songs such as "We Don't Want to Fight Wars No More," which was played widely on TV and radio when the Nigerian–Cameroon conflict broke out. Afro-English bands like Orchestra Jazira have made a point of singing antiwar songs, and their declared aims are peace and unity. Similarly, Miriam Makeba, when in England in 1985, made verbal and sung pleas for peace—with integral equality for black people.

American singers have long used music as a medium seeking equality and peace as interlocking aims. Curtis Mayfield has always been one of the most clear-sighted and cogently articulate of black spokesmen, and his "Got to Have Peace" projects prevailing attitudes very straightforwardly. He sees peace as essential "to keep the world alive" and to "save the children."[2]

Afrikaa Bambaataa and John Lydon have denounced war on a rap and disco record, and Bambaataa and James Brown have made a lengthy single together that denounces war as antilife and destructive of unity, peace, beauty, or love.[3] Bob Marley denounced wars in the United States and the Caribbean as ways of exploiting black people and setting them against their natural allies, the Indians.[4] Steel Pulse, a reggae band from Birmingham, England, has made several attacks on war. "Soldiers," on the album *Handsworth Revolution* (Island ILPS 9502, 1978), is one of the most eloquent:

> Is there a need for war?
> No
> Peace my bredren—hear them bawl
> Bodies in mutilated condition
> Faces scarred beyond recognition
> Is this what civilization means to me?
> Then without it I prefer to be.

Eddy Grant adds humor to his denunciation of the misuse of war as black and Indian genocide in "War Party."[5]

Such cynicism was prevalent as far back as the days of the American Civil War. Obviously there were slaves who saw the war as a battle for their freedom and sang about it as such, but far more were wise enough to understand that this was not a war fought specifically to obtain emancipation, although it would nevertheless result in the end of slavery. This pragmatism was evident in a popular slave song of the Civil War years:

> Don't see the lightning flashing in the canebrakes,
> Looks like we gonna have a storm
> Although you're mistaken it's the Yankee soldiers
> Going to fight for Uncle Sam
> Old master was a colonel in the Rebel army
> Just before he had to run away—
> Look out for the battle is a-falling
> The darkies gonna occupy the land.[6]

Even as the war ended, few songs celebrated the actual war or the victory of the North; they simply rejoiced in blacks' freedom and in the demotion of their masters, as with "O Massa a rebel, we row him to prison."[7] The most popular songs of the time gave thanks that black people were "free at last" and that

Slavery chain done broke at last!
Broke at last! Broke at last!
Slavery chain done broke at last!
Gonna praise God till I die![8]

One of the first major wars to heavily involve black soldiers from the United States, Britain, and British colonies was World War I. The songs written by black people about the impact of the war reflected the ambivalence inherent in the situation. This was a war that created jobs for black people. In the United States, for instance, it sparked a massive migration from the South to northern cities where war industries were clamoring for cheap labor even before the United States actually declared war on Germany in 1917. It was also a war that was fought, ostensibly, for democratic principles. Black soldiers went to the front with high hopes that racism in their own countries would be defeated at the same time as German fascism. Such optimism and the concomitant disillusionment when racism continued to thrive after the war were reflected in contemporary songs. Some blues and calypso idealized the war, but more were cast in the realistic mold of Blind Willie Johnson's 1929 retrospective blues "When the War Was On." Blind Willie talks not only about the allied victory over the Germans but also about the rationing and hardship. He acerbically comments on the continuing segregation in the armed forces themselves—a segregation that was reinforced by "President Wilson sitting on a throne" and "making law for everyone."[9]

One of Bessie Smith's best selling records, "Poor Man's Blues," also recorded in 1929, refers to World War I as a theoretically leveling experience that actually left extremes of poverty and wealth in its wake.[10] Sister Kelly Fancy goes even further into dire pessimism in her 1931 song "Death Is Riding Through the Land" when she predicts that the inadequacy of the peace settlement will rapidly lead to another world war.[11]

World War II aroused the same mixture of support, indifference, and rejection. Some black people were aware that the war pulled the United States out of the Depression; others saw the war as a moral crusade against an inhuman fascist advance. A few black leaders and activists hoped that the inequality that prevailed in employment could be more effectively tackled in a time of war-induced expansion and national solidarity. Before and during the Depression black people had been last hired and first fired. Philip Randolph, the black leader of the Union of Sleeping Car Porters and the editor of *The Black Worker*, attempted to induce the government to introduce equal employment in government-controlled industries. When threatened with a march on Washington of 100,000 black people in 1941, President Franklin Delano Roosevelt did agree to set up the Fair Employment Practices Commission. This led to very little tangible improvement, but the war itself did create more jobs, and many more black soldiers joined the army and fought in Europe than had been the case in World War I.

Perhaps because such a large number of black soldiers were involved, blues singers often saw war as a disaster that would lead to personal loss and tragedy. Lightnin' Hopkins links the onset of the war to the loss of a child when, on December 7, 1941, the Japanese bombed Pearl Harbor: "Oh Lord, they bomb my baby chile."[12] The fear of death springs to Champion Jack Dupree's mind when he hears the news about Pearl Harbor. He listens to President Roosevelt's speech and thinks of all the young men who will be called up and be sent to their deaths. Leadbelly makes a firm decision that he will not be one of those—when his girl asks him to go down to the "Red Cross Store" and enlist, he refuses, because in this war there is "nothing to fight for. . . . I ain' playing in no rich man's show."[13] In a similar vein, Bukka White is determined to avoid the draft—even if it means pretending to be mentally incompetent:

> When Uncle Sam take all your men and boys to war,
> I'm goin' be jes' like a coon.[14]

He, like Brownie McGee in a "Million Lonesome Women," can see all the advantages to being one of the few men left around so many women whose husbands are away in the armed forces.

When patriotism did surface, it was sincere and wholehearted. Leadbelly shows he can sing about both sides of a situation in the blues "Tear Hitler Down." To Buster "Buzz" Ezell, Hitler was the direct enemy of racial equality: "treating us so mean with his dreadful submarines so his land can be enlarged."[15] Dr. Clayton similarly denounced the Germans and the Japanese in "Pearl Harbor Blues."

To Son House the issues were clear-cut enough to make him convinced that

> You ought to do everything that you can
> We got to win this war.[16]

In songs like "We Got to Win" and "War Time Blues," Sonny Boy Williamson (John Lee Williamson) not only agrees but goes much further: "I want to drop the bomb and set the Japanese city on fire" and "because they are so rotten, I just love to see them die."[17] The Percy Wilborn Quartet was convinced that the Allies won the war "Because God was on our side."[18]

For some people, like Florida Kid, in his "Hitler Blues," the war can be used as a bizarre way of getting the woman he lusts after to sleep with him. His logic is that because "Hitler, he's a bad man," she ought to console Florida Kid in bed. Maybe it's just an elemental juxtapositioning of love with hate! Louis Jordan's "G.I. Blues" was equally light but more obviously humorous, and it sailed into the top 10 in 1944.[19] On "You Can't Do That No More," Jordan offers far more trenchant, though still witty, comments on changes brought about by the war.

As the war ended, any euphoria rapidly disappeared, and many were left with J. D. Short's cynical sense of puzzlement over the issues that had been at stake. He simply did not know what it had all been about.[20] Big Bill Broonzy resented the fact that black soldiers had been fighting overseas for the principles of democracy and equality and yet still were treated as less than men on their return to the United States. He plaintively asked "When Will I Get to be Called a Man?"[21] Socially, black people were still segregated and usually had to accept inferior schooling, transportation, and recreational facilities. In the South, black voters had been totally disenfranchised since the start of the century, and were to remain so through the next decade. All the campaigners for fair employment had won only a token success. The Fair Employment Practices Commission had had a minimal impact on industrial segregation and unequal pay and conditions. It is hardly surprising that so few songs saw World War II as likely to improve the position of black people in white society.

Black soldiers flooded into Europe from the British colonies. In particular West Indian soldiers fought in British regiments and sang patriotic songs denouncing Hitler and his inegalitarian fascist regime.

Years later Eek-a-Mouse, the highly original Jamaican DJ singer, echoed some of the West Indian attitudes to Hitler that had been formulated during the war when he sang about Hitler as a dangerous psychopath who needed to be eliminated.[22] Popular West Indian songs of the time went on to reflect a disillusionment with the war similar to that experienced in the United States. In Britain, as in the United States, returning black soldiers were treated as inferior citizens and encouraged to return to the West Indies. In both countries, it was clear that fighting for democracy was no ticket to equality for black people.

The horror of the way in which the war against Japan was won courses through black songs of the time like a shock wave. In 1946 a popular black gospel group, The Golden Gate Quartet, recorded "Atom and Evil," which compares the atom bomb to original sin. Slim Gaillard's "Atomic Cocktail" is, in contrast, a far less serious equation of the atomic bomb with controlling power. It lacks the sense of menace that colors the awesome song "Red's Dream," recorded by Louisiana Red in 1962, which is filled with an eight year old's impression of frightening devastation. A still more specific warning against the misuse of atomic power is powerfully delivered by the Spirit of Memphis Quartet on "Atomic Telephone."[23] Hiroshima and Nagasaki had made people realize that warfare had become a different and more destructive kind of game.

Only a few years of peace intervened before the United States was plunged into the Korean War. J. B. Lenoir sees it as an unpleasant but God-given mission to fight in Korea.[24] The most moving song about Korea is Lightnin' Hopkins' "Sad News from Korea." There is no homage paid to the gallantry of soldiers or the godliness of causes; here the misery caused by lost lives is the focus. A mother cries over her missing son—"Send my poor child back to me." War is seen as a tragedy and a waste.[25]

Vietnam was a very different sort of war. It crept up on most Americans through sudden extensions of the draft and unexpected deaths in the family. Nonetheless, even the war that was waged to uphold the precarious power of a regime of dubious popularity in a small Southeast Asian country inspired a minor wave of patriotic fervor. "Greetings (This Is Uncle Sam)," by The Monitors in 1966 (V.P. 25032), and "Forget-Me-Not" by Martha and The Vandellas in 1968 (Gordy 7070), made responding positively to the draft seem like a noble act. Reluctance to go to war rapidly became endemic, as John Lee Hooker summed up:

Sittin' here thinkin', thinkin', thinkin', I don't wanna
  go to Vietnam.
United States have so much trouble of their own, why
  they wanna fight in Vietnam?
Lord have mercy, don't let me go to Vietnam
Lord have mercy, Lord have mercy, don't let me go to Vietnam
I have my wife and my family, I don't wanna go to Vietnam.

We got so much trouble at home, we don't need to go to Vietnam
Yeah, yeah, we got all of our troubles right here at home,
  don't need to go to Vietnam.[26]

Leon Thomas went beyond John Lee Hooker's disinclination to go to Vietnam with his "Damn Nam (Ain't Goin' to Vietnam)." He, like those who rejected the draft, was refusing to go to war, and he was condemning the ethos as well as the actuality of the struggle in Vietnam. To him it was a "dirty mean war," and he was not going to Vietnam.[27]

Those men who were called up and fought in Vietnam express loathing and distaste for the whole war. Luther Allison is called up, and it's "Bad News." Bobbly Bland wakes up screaming, dreaming about the horror of Vietnam, when he comes home on leave from the army in 1963.[28]

The legitimacy of the war in Vietnam is questioned by Marvin Gaye in one of the most outstanding records of all time. Recorded in 1969, *What's Goin' On* raised uncomfortable questions not only about the war but also about its impact on American society. The haunting lyrics were given directional drive by the compulsive beat and memorable melodies. The record had such enormous sales that the ideas it floated must have lingered in the minds of millions of people.[29] Freddie Hubbard's attack on the waste and injustice of the Vietnam War was a mixture of arresting jazz and a recited poem about being a "Black Soldier." *Sing me a Song of Songmy* obviously had more limited appeal than *What's Goin' On*, but was a powerful and strident indictment of such horrific incidents as My Lai.[30] Junior Wells made a more personal but equally intense indictment of Vietnam when he sang "Vietcong Blues." A letter from his brother who was fighting in Vietnam nearly drove him out of his mind with anguish and anger, because he told Junior that he had "no reason to fight."[31] It was at much the same time that Edwin Starr had his no. 1 hit in *Billboards* pop charts with *War*. He followed that up with *Stop the War Now*, which was recorded later in 1970. Freda Payne joined the antiwar campaign in 1971 with *Bring the Boys Home*, and in 1974 the Chi Lites and O. C. Smith made pleas for peace with *There Will Never Be Any Peace (Until God Is Seated at the Conference Table)*.[32]

Bernice Reagon, lead singer of Sweet Honey in the Rock as well an acclaimed solo artist, celebrated the Vietnamese victory in 1975 as a triumph for liberation with the song "There's a New World Coming."[33] The Last Poets did much the same with "Ho Chi Minh," but in a more elliptical fashion.[34] Jimmy Cliff, however, stood outside the conflict as a concerned West Indian and sang powerfully about the tragic loss, and the needless death and destruction, of such a catastrophic war.[35]

The specter of a holocaustic war has hung over the world ever since Hiroshima and Nagasaki demonstrated the long-term devastation inherent in the use of the atom bomb. There is now the constant fear that even a small, apparently containable, war could escalate into a conflict in which nuclear bombs might be used. Songs for peace and songs that attack the stupidity and waste of war are all, to a greater or lesser extent, directed at this fearsome possibility. Barbara Mason voiced the universal fear in 1974 when she sang that if people keep resorting to violence and war, the world "soon will be rubble."[36] Stevie Wonder echoed her sentiments and sang on "Higher Ground" that the world will not keep on turning much longer if governments keep on lying while their people are dying.[37] A few years later he played harmonica on a Brenda Russell album, *Two Eyes*, on which one of the strongest tracks, "Look Down, Young Soldier," predicted total devastation if wars did not end.[38] The Womacks, Cecil and Linda, think that every singer and every politician should denounce war. "We definitely identify with peace, it's the only way human society will survive."[39]

Strong antiwar songs have come out of groups that straddle musical genres. Jazz-rock and jazz-funk groups have made some of the most compelling pleas for peace. The jazz-rock funk group War creates an eerie sense of doom and desolation in "World War III" on the album *Life (Is So Strange)*. The fearful air of menace is so strong in this song that the most unconcerned listener is likely to come face to face with the awesome likelihood of destruction by nuclear war.[40]

The jazz musician Sun Ra, who cannot be put into any musical category, has made a single specifically denouncing nuclear war; in it the ominous words "nuclear war" are repeated in a dark, brooding tone. Sun Ra also has organized simultaneous antiwar concerts over the world and has said, "If a lot of musicians got together simple for survival [sic] of this planet, whoever owns this planet will be compelled to say 'There's something of worth on this planet, I'm not gonna destroy it.'"[41] This 72-year-old creator of some of the most startling and dissonant music around is determined to try and use that music to bring the world to its senses.

Funk jazzman Joe Bowie is more skeptical. Even though one of his most impressive albums with his band, Defunkt, is called *Thermo-Nuclear Sweat*, and he has rearranged the song of that name from his first album, he thinks "It'd be nice if we could do something about it, but I don't think we can, because of the way the governments, the world, is structured. See, the people who *make* nuclear war ain't going to be hit by it in the same way as the rest of us. And the people who cry out against it are the ones who do the fighting basically, either economically or physically. So its kinda hard to change all the people who have all the money and all the control, either way they're still gonna be cool. It's impossible, I believe, for us to get rid of the threat unless we get rid of those people first." Yet Bowie still considers it worth attempting to influence minds and hearts through music: "I mean, I'd like to get a record out about it before the war itself. It gets an even more pressing issue with each day that passes, with all the cold wars we've got, and getting hotter. I really do believe we're moving towards nuclear disaster, quickly."[42]

Other luminaries of jazz funk, such as Lonnie Liston Smith, have made impassioned pleas for peace, and masters of go-go funk, such as Trouble Funk, perform and record devastating satires on war and bombs like "Drop the Bomb." More direct and carefully aimed are rap records such as Grandmaster Melle Mel and The Furious Five's "World War III." Such numbers are unambivalently designed to involve people in the heavy dance beat and then bombard them with the practical common sense of doing everything they can to avoid a nuclear-centered World War III.[43] Equally significantly, early rap artists such as Gil Scott-Heron have consistently warned of the likelihood of nuclear war and the dangers of nuclear energy. The godfather of soul-funk fusion has joined up with Afrikaa Bambaataa to attack nuclear warfare. When interviewed in 1984, James Brown said, "Yeah, the message is clear and concerns itself with the fight against nuclear war. I'm not making any political statement as such, I'm simply inviting the people to be on their guard against the possibility of a nuclear war. The song is a statement for peace from myself and Afrikaa Bambaataa."[44]

James Brown was one of the American R&B singers who sparked the evolution of reggae in Jamaica in the 1950s and 1960s. By the 1970s and 1980s reggae artists were at one with James Brown in denouncing nuclear war and the political stands and attitudes likely to lead to such a war. It is fascinating that such a strong condemnation of nuclear war exists in the West Indies. Obviously Americans would feel a strong concern and fear, since their country would be a prime target in any attack made by Russia as the other dominant super-power. Fallout from the United States would likely spill over into the West Indies. However, the admonitions for peace in reggae songs are both a reflection of a philosophical belief in the superiority of a peaceful attitude and a deep-rooted fear that irresponsible politicians will initiate nuclear destruction.

In the 1970s, U-Roy, The Ethiopians, The Royals, The Wailing Souls, The Twinkle Brothers, Tapper Zukie, The Mighty Diamonds, and, of course, Bob Marley and The Wailers all urged peace rather than war on alienated governments. By the 1980s Dennis Brown was foretelling a nuclear "Amargideon."[45] The hugely popular DJs Clint Eastwood and General Saint were demanding "Stop That Train," leaving no doubt that they meant the nuclear train to destruction. They usually added humor to their already potent arguments, but on "Nuclear Crisis," their alienated, doom-ridden lyrics are given mournful intensity by the jazz-funk-inflected experimental rhythms. With verve and style Eastwood and Saint compare the horrors of World War I and World War II with the likely extermination of the human race if politicians go on heading for World War III:

> World War 1 it was the bouncing bomb
> World War 2 Hitler kill off the Jew
> World War 3 them ago kill everybody
> Everything in the land and everything in de sea
>
> The women them put on a demonstration.
> If it take all me strength and all me energy
> I will even die for this country
> Beware, cos we no want nuclear. Beware.[46]

A year or so later Eastwood and Saint, who proclaimed that they wanted to write lyrics with universal significance, wrote the even gloomier "Can't Take Another World War," which is on their album *Two Bad DJs*: "The whole world gone to atomic bomb." They see the only solution as a ban on the neutron bomb. Eastwood and Saint were both born in Jamaica but had settled in England by the time these records were made.

Third World is a British reggae band with strong Jamaican roots. They have used R&B, jazz, funk, rock guitar riffs, and even a classical cello in their repertoire. Their "Third World War" is as disturbing lyrically as it is complex musically. There is an explicit urgency in the lyrics and an implicit dynamic in the music that make this one of the most powerful antinuclear war songs. Other British-based reggae artists and acts—Winston Reedy, Eddy Grant, Linton Kwesi Johnson, Carroll Thompson, Steel Pulse, Misty-in-Roots, and Aswad—have appealed for sanity to prevail over the power mania that leads to such irreversible catastrophe. Atomic power is denounced by Natalie Xavier as inextricably linked to the atomic bomb; it will lead "people to destruction."[47]

African bands who sing in English are not numerous, but those who do are vocal in their denunciation of nuclear warfare. Their fears are voiced by one of Nigeria's greatest musicians and most lauded superstars. To Sunny Ade such a war is the preeminent threat of mankind:

I have a fear which plays on my mind. It's that these nuclear bombs around us might explode at any time which is mad, because even those who make them will never survive. This generation of African countries are known as the Third World. And if people know the Third World is coming up, why would they want to perish it? Nuclear bombs, if let off, would mean the Third World would no longer exist. That's my fear.[48]

George Lee, leader of the Mozambique band Anansi attempts to change the direction of world leadership with his "Song of Peace." Certainly the hypnotic optimism of his mellow saxophone is seductive enough to have some influence on anyone who listens.[49] But even George Lee is aware that world leaders have the most difficult minds to change. Like most musicians he hopes to affect those among the general public who are open to new ideas and influences; they, in turn, may help create a general shift in the climate of world opinion about nuclear bombs and future wars.

Follo Graff, the lead singer of the multiethnic, multinationality, London-based African band Orchestra Jazira, passionately believes that music can change people's minds and opinions. He uses song to build people's defenses against "war" and "supernuclear radiation."[50]

NOTES

1. Edwin Starr, *War*, Gordy 7101 (1970).

2. Curtis Mayfield, *Roots*, Buddah Super 2318/045 (1971).

3. Afrikaa Bambaataa and James Brown, *Unity*, Polydor AFRX 2 (1984).

4. Bob Marley, "Buffalo Soldiers," *Confrontation*, Island ILPS 9760 (1983).

5. Eddy Grant, "War Party," *Killer on the Rampage*, ICE LP 3023 (1983).

6. George Rawick, ed., *The American Slave: A Composite Autobiography*, XVII, *Florida Narratives* (Westport, CT: Greenwood Press, 1972), pp. 161–162.

7. Leon Litwack, *Been in the Storm So Long: The Aftermath of Slavery* (London: Athlone Press, 1979), p. 153.

8. Litwack, *Storm*, p. 169.

9. "Aspects of the Blues," pt. IV, "War," Radio 3, March 5, 1980.

10. Bessie Smith, *Empty Bed Blues*, CBS 66273.

11. "Aspects of the Blues," pt. IV, "War," Radio 3, March 5, 1980.

12. Lightnin' Hopkins, "Dec. 7 1941," *Soul: in the Beginning*, Sun 6467251.

13. Huddie Ledbetter (Leadbelly), "Red Cross Store," *The Saga of Leadbelly*, Melodisc MLP 12-107.

14. Bukka White, "Army Blues," in A. X. Nicholas, ed., *Woke up This Morning: Poetry of the Blues* (New York: Bantam, 1973), p. 75.

15. Buster "Buzz" Ezell, "Roosevelt and Hitler," *Fort Valley Blues*, Matchbox SDM 260.

16. Son House, "American Defense," *The Legendary Son House, 1941–2 Recordings*, Roots Special Edition RSE 1.

17. Sonny Boy Williamson (John Lee), "War Time Blues," *Sonny Boy Williamson*, Vol. 1, Bluebird No. 1, RCA 7203.

18. Percy Wilborn Quartet, "Oh, What a Time," *A Treasury of Field Recordings*, Vol. 2, 77 Records 77 LA-12-3.

19. Peter Hesbacher and Less Waffen, "War Recordings: Incidence and Change (1940–1970)," *Popular Music and Society*, 8, nos. 3 and 4 (1982): Appendix, p. 90.

20. J. D. Short, "Fighting for Dear Old Sam," *Delta Blues*, Xtra 1080.

21. Big Bill Broonzy, "When Will I Get to Be Called a Man," in Nicholas, ed., *Woke up*, p. 47.

22. Eek-a-Mouse, "Hitler," *The Mouse and the Man*, Greensleeves GREL 56 (1983).

23. *Atomic Cafe*, Rounder 1034.

24. J. B. Lenoir, *J. B. Lenoir*, Chess Bluemaster Series 2 A CMB 208.

25. "Aspects of the Blues," Pt. IV, "War," Radio 3, March 5, 1980.

26. John Lee Hooker, "I Don't Wanna Go to Vietnam," *Tantalizing with the Blues*, MCA MCL 1986.

27. Rap Brown and Leon Thomas, *Flying Dutchman*, FDS 136 (1970).

28. Luther Allison, *Bad News Is Coming*, Vogue VG 407 523023; Bobby "Blue" Bland, *Woke up Screaming*, Ace CH41.

29. Marvin Gaye, *What's Goin' On*, TAM T5-310.

30. Freddie Hubbard, *Sing Me a Song of Songmy*, Atlantic ALL 50255 (1971).

31. Junior Wells, Chicago Blues Band, J. B. Hutto and His Hawks, Otis Spann's South Side Piano, *Chicago/The Blues/Today*, Vol. 1, Vanguard VSD 79216 (1972).

32. Edwin Starr, *War*, Gordy 7101 (1970) and *Stop the War Now*, Gordy 7104 (1970); Freda Payne, *Bring the Boys Home*, Invictus 9092 (1971); Chi Lites, *There Will Never Be* (etc.), Brunswick 55512 (1974); O. C. Smith, *La La Peace Song*, Columbia 10031 (1974).

33. Bernice Reagon, *Give Your Hands to Struggle*, Paredon Records P-1028 (1975).

34. Last Poets, *Delights of the Garden*, Casa LP 7051 (1977).

35. Jimmy Cliff, *Jimmy Cliff: Reggae Greats*, Island IRG 14 (1985).

36. Barbara Mason, "World in a Crisis," *Transitions* PYE B DLP 4027 (1974).

37. Stevie Wonder, *Innervisions*, Tamla Motown STMA 8011 (1973).

38. Brenda Russell, *Two Eyes*, Warner RCA (1983).

39. Stuart Cosgrove, "A Family Affair," *New Musical Express*, October 5, 1985, p. 15.

40. War, *Life (Is So Strange)* RCA 250 SA (1983).

41. Sun Ra, *Nuclear War*, Y Records RA 1; Lynden Barber, "The Joy of Life," *Melody Maker*, November 19, 1983, p. 31.

42. Chris May, "Three Minute Warnings: Defunkt," *Black Music*, June 1982, p. 21.

43. Grandmaster Melle Mel and The Furious 5, *Stepping Off*, Sugarhill SH LP 5555 (1985).

44. Malu Halasa, "Meeting of The Minds," *Blues and Soul*, no. 414 (1984): 9.

45. Dennis Brown, "*Armagideon*," Tads (1984).

46. Clint Eastwood and General Saint, *Stop That Train*, Greensleeves GREL 53 (1983).

47. Natalie Xavier, *Atomic Energy*, People Unite Musicians Cooperative PU/NAT 001 (1983).

48. Jack Barron, "Synch or Swim," *Sounds*, July 9, 1983, p. 22.

49. George Lee's Anansi, *Anansi*, Ebusia (1985).

50. Interview with author at Commonwealth Institute Gardens, Holland Park, London, August 22, 1983.

8 *The Music and the Message*

Black music has been a collective cry of discontent for as long as there have been situations and conditions in need of change. Songs spring out of a broad cultural context and represent a wide range of people. The message of the lyrics is usually complemented or enhanced by the underlying musical patterns. The effectiveness of the melody or the rhythm can have a dynamically significant effect on the impact that number has on a listener.

Ron Welburn, a black American writer, said, "Our music is the foremost expressive quality of our being, black music describes and celebrates life through black people. The degree to which we shape our music and protect it will dictate the full range and extent of our survival in the United States." He has also asserted that the "black musician is ahead of everyone in the expression of true black sensibility." But his most dramatic statement must surely be that "Our music is our key to survival."[1] It is also a key to unlock the door of change.

The majority of black people in most Western countries are in dire need of change. In the United States, for instance, black employment is still far below that of whites as far as the numbers actually employed and the kind of jobs and remuneration they obtain.

Any hope that the political arena will provide solutions in countries such as the United States is slim. It was not until the 1960s that all black Americans regained the right to vote and to be elected that was officially received 100 years earlier. What has this led to? Admittedly there are now 5,000 black elected officials instead of the mere hand-ful that existed before the great surge of black voters to the polls in the wake of the 1964 Civil Rights Act and 1965 Voting Rights Act. But how much power do these disproportionately few officials have? Most are in minor, noninfluential positions, and those who have become mayors are constrained by the lack of funds that blights inner city centers, unable to draw on the middle class, taxable wealth of the suburbs. Congress is hardly an arena where hopes for black equality can be focused. The maximum black membership of the House of Representatives since the mid-1960s has hovered around 20. That is hardly enough to form a pressure group—never mind to swing signifi-cantly legislation—and it is undoubtedly a disproportionately low percentage of the House, when 11 to 14 percent of the population at large is black. The situation in the Senate is even worse. There has been only one black senator in recent decades, and he may well have been discredited by what black Congressman Ronald Dellums has called a vicious saga of victimization of black politicians.

Music, rather than politics, has provided the real voice of black America. To William McClendon, director of black studies at Reed College in Portland, Oregon:

Black music is a lasting symbol of sanity for black people . . . closely related to the spirit of resistance and struggle . . . It is one of the effective modes of communication for conveying the messages of black abhorrence and resis-tance to the repressive living arrangements created for black people. Black music is an amalgam of black life . . . an indigenous expression of collective black experience.[2]

Bobby "Blue" Bland has, in "Lead Me On" (*Two Steps from the Blues*, Duke X-74), aptly expressed the black American dilemma—wanting to be accepted as equals in the American dream, blacks are treated as strangers in the land of their birth:

You know how it feels—you understand
What it is to be a stranger, in this unfriendly land.

Bobby Bland also has stressed the role of music in creating a more positive climate.[3] Blues has always been a music of protest, a cry of pain, and an articulation of black anger; jazz rapidly took on a parallel role, and by the 1960s the music often incorporated so strong a sense of directed agitation that when words were added, they were a reinforcement rather than a necessity. In both music and lyrics Max Roach and Oscar Brown, Jr., created a work of such radicalism and brilliance when they wrote the "Freedom Now Suite" that they helped to further the quest for black equality in the United States. First performed in 1960, it has been described as "imbued with the beat of that young movement in the U.S. and with the new consciousness arising in Africa." It helped "to educate, inspire and point the way."[4]

In Britain the black political scene can only be described as a national disgrace. Not until 1987 were there any black members of the House of Commons. One of the earlier more esteemed but unsuccessful parliamentary candidates was finally given a place in the House of Lords, but the solitary black face of Lord Pitt and four new black members of the House of Commons can hardly affect the destiny of what is now over 5 percent of the British population. As in most other countries, black people have the highest proportion of unemployed and the worst level of pay. They still face discrimination in all areas of life.

The most impressive among the efforts to use music to alter this racist state of affairs was made in the late 1970s. Rock Against Racism was a genuinely radical movement. Inspired by the Socialist Workers Party, it fought prejudice in a very direct way. Whenever a National Front rally was announced, the possibility of whipping up anti-black, pro-fascist feeling was denied by Rock Against Racism, who would arrange a carnival or concert of black and white people to direct energy and enthusiasm into more appropriate channels. Punk bands played alongside reggae bands, and many groups who could not easily be categorized had a black and white lineup. The previously bland Cimarons, with lead singer Winston Reedy, sang and recorded the clarion call number "Rock Against Racism" (Polydor CIMA 12, 1979). Their sound was sharpened to a menacing cutting edge, and the heavy rhythm resonated around the hard-hitting lyrics. Rock Against Racism was not just a British attempt to minimize the impact of a racist society on black Britons; it was a socialist effort to revolutionize that society so that racism would become as redundant as it was reprehensible.

Since that unique period in the late 1970s, British bands have continued to use reggae as a positive force for change. In the 1980s Abacush writes and sings about a wide range of social and political problems in Britain. It said in an interview with this author, "We are writing from our own experiences and we believe that music can express a sense of the world as it is and as it can be changed . . . we want to speak for and to the world at large. We want to express what people feel. Music is a basic form of communication between people."[5]

Music has always been a basically elemental force for change in Jamaica. Edward Seaga was so aware of this that his prepolitical career revolved around record production; but once he was a politician, he found that he could not control the spontaneous flow of critical comment that sprang from reggae singers. Jamaica is still suffering from a corrupt political system and the inordinate exploitation of poverty-stricken black people. Singers have long been among the activists determined to transform this unacceptable way of life. Bob Marley saw himself as indistinguishable from the music of rebellion. He sang "I, rebel music" in "Them Belly Full (But We Hungry)" (*Natty Dread*, Island ILPS 9281, 1974). And he was determined to "free our people with music" ("Trench Town," *Confrontation*, Bland/Tuff Gong, ILPS 9760, 1983). To him, music was a sword wielded in the cause of justice, and a weapon that was powerful enough to produce a real transformation in politics and patterns of living.

Michael Smith, the radical dub poet who died in 1983, once said that through poetry and music people could become more aware of "a way forward for their ultimate liberation." Lincoln Thompson believes the message in reggae is essentially one of liberation, and the "music has got to play and our voice has still got to be heard."[6]

Almost all the causes of pain, misery, and anger for deprived people are covered by Leroy Sibbles in "Life in the Ghetto" (*Strictly Roots*, Micron Miccas 0038, 1981). The heavy dominance of the bass and drums allows the fluid voice to flow over the rhythm, and to make every word bounce into the listener's mind. The intention is obviously to move people to act in such a way that a stagnant situation will become dynamic and open to real transformation.

I-Roy is one of the Jamaican sound system operators and toasters whose concerns have revolved about the state of the world. In song Roy Reid (his real name) has often been prophetic as well as wise. He has said:

My inspirations are deep down within me, it's something that I see in everyday life. I see segregation, I see sufferation, I see annihilation. . . . I see the margin between and it goes on and on. When I go into the studio it all comes out, I don't even have to write out lyrics beforehand. . . . I'm trying to reach out and touch the people who are so far away and who live in a world of fantasy, they can't even take this time off to see what they're made of, you know.[7]

Nigeria has seen a succession of repressive black regimes over the last decade or so, and musicians have sought to encourage people to seek a reduction in autocratic rule and improvement in living standards. Sunny Ade's aim is to sing about the problems of modern life in Nigeria and "to have as beneficial effect as possible on the largest number of people."[8] More aggressive and unremitting in his demands, Fela Anikulapo Kuti is as famous as a revolutionary as he is as a musician. John Collins said of Fela that "his blunt anti-establishment lyrics have made him the Bob Dylan and Mick Jagger of Africa." His Afro-beat has indeed become archetypal revolutionary music. It is difficult to regard it just as music: it has become too obviously the foundation for a political movement. On tour Fela has adopted the slogan "Music Is the Weapon of the Future," and believes his music is the basis for returning political power to the people.[9] To Nigerian Sunny Okosun, "a musician is a lecturer," and he feels it fitting to "sing protest songs and songs of truth."[10]

Ever since the introduction of apartheid, it has been essential for black South Africans to use every possible weapon in the struggle against inequality and discrimination. Despite attempts by the Boer governments to destroy cultural coherence among black people, music has been a powerful force for uniting minds and hearts, policies and plans, resistance and rebellion among the oppressed masses.

Music is one of the South African performing arts that continue "to play an active role in the evolution of black identity and the internal definition of black aspirations in South Africa."[11] Musicians, David Coplan is convinced, are among those who have given the struggle for black self-determination "an indispensible cultural vitality." He stresses the importance of the music as well as the lyrics in building and retaining a sense of cultural pride and autonomy. No song with subversive lyrics can be played on the radio, but "political, socially relevant, authentic township music" continues to be produced. Anti-apartheid bands like The Minerals get records like their "Sweet Soweto" popularized by the record shops and word-of-mouth recommendation. Bands like the Malombo Jazz Men that used radically political, poetic chanting and actively supported the black consciousness movement were always torn by the need to support the revolutionary impulse and the knowledge that publicly doing so would result in restraint by the government. Julian Bahula, for instance, was a member of this band in the 1960s and of Malombo Jazz Makers in the 1970s; and when attention began to focus on their presence at radical student rallies, he was among those who were forced into exile.[12] Other bands that truthfully depict the deprivations of exploitation suffered by black South Africans—bands like Sakhile and Harare—have survived government criticism and still put out anticolonial records such as Harare's *Kalahari Rock* (Gallo ML4303).

In South Africa, musicians who are critical of the government, or of the way of life that the government imposes, are put onto vinyl by small, independent record companies. There is no danger that they will be subsumed by the system. Elsewhere, especially in Britain and the United States, there is always the risk that lyrics will be examined by the large record companies, frightened of repercussions if they allow antiestablishment views through the net. As Dave Harker has pointed out, it is diffcult for even the most radical musicians not to get co-opted into the system, but it is possible to remain independent and critical. In Britain, Rock Against Racism is the best example of such success; in the United States there has never been such a coherently organized movement.[13] There it is individual singers or bands who have retained their autonomy, and their ability to question and condemn. Sometimes this is a freedom won only when their records are put out on their own labels; at other times singer/songwriters like Marvin Gaye and Gil Scott-Heron have demanded, and usually won, their freedom to write and sing without constraint.

One talented black musician, Donald Byrd, is aware of all the commercial pressure that can mold music, but he is still convinced that black music springs so essentially from the people that it can, and does, retain its role as their authentic voice.[14]

Bluesmen captured the essence of black American dreams, as well as despair over situations that were localized and problems that were universal. Some sang with such bitter pain that there could be no doubt about their moving truthfulness. One afternoon in 1942, for instance, a record was made that came from the gut of black experience and was in no way responding to or curtailed by the needs or demands of any record company. Son House was given the afternoon off from working on his plantation to record for the Library of Congress. In Klak's General Store, a source of local credit and despair, in Robinsville, Mississippi, Alan Lomax put down half a dozen inimitable tracks. They included a song that summed up over half a century's exploitation and frustration. "Country Farm Blues" encapsulated all the shattered hopes and abiding faith in the value of working on the land that tore black people apart in those years around the turn of the twentieth century. More specifically, Son House sang his "only protest at the harsh farm-gang system that has brutalized the lives of himself and the men in the lonely countryside around him. It is the reality that hung around the poor cabin where he lived, like the drifting smoke from a dying autumn fire."[15] In that same session Son House also conveyed black America's reluctance to fight an external war for democracy while being denied democratic rights at home. The album was a multifaceted mirror that reflected so many of the fears and aspirations of black Americans in the 1940s. It was not untypical, and was certainly not an isolated example of blues representing raw human reactions.

More than two decades later, "Born Under a Bad Sign" delves deeply into the sources of black anger and discontent. Several blues singers have recorded excellent versions of this song that lists illiteracy, poverty, and general bad luck as basic handicaps in an overly competitive society; but it is Albert King's rough, emotional voice and earthy blues guitar that have produced the most disturbing and tragic version (*King of the Blues Guitar*, Atco 8213). This again is a tough denunciation of the fate of most black Americans that has somehow slipped by record companies anxious not to seem to allow their artists to attack the system that supports them.

At much the same time, Louisiana Red went as far as to say that black singers and musicians would do a far better job of running the country than the current crop of politicians. He saw in "Red's Dream," a Senate dominated by Ray Charles, Lightnin' Hopkins, Jimmy Reed, Bo Diddley, and Big Maybelle. He himself walked into the United Nations and set "the whole nation right" before he ordered Khrushchev to get all the Soviet missiles out of Cuba.

Modern black music has obviously inherited a spirit of rebellion from blues. The protest by subtle and humorous innuendo, as much as by obvious criticism, was a tradition that had abounded in the 1920s and was perfected by Louis Jordan in the 1940s. Chuck Berry carried it through into rock and roll with a wit that was never so evidently cutting that it could not be seen as acceptable. He created music for young rebels, and as a bluesman he stood firmly outside the mainstream, always conscious that he was a critical outsider. Neither he nor any of the early black progenitors of rock and roll, such as Bo Diddley, Fats Domino, or Little Richard, ever had the kind of success that could make them respectable members of the establishment. None of them ever got rich, and none of them was molded by the industry. Since those early heady days it has become more difficult to separate the role of black music as an articulator of dangerous protest from music as mere catharsis. It is possible to see all recent black music as catering to the needs of the capitalistic music industry, with its most subversive lyrics carrying no more real menace than a wet dream. It is more reasonable, however, to recognize that there is a continuing spirit of rebellion in much of today's music.

Roy Ayers is among those who believe that music really can help bring about change. He thinks music can start revolutions in the hearts and minds of people everywhere: "At this point in my life as a musician and a black man, I feel that I have to use my talents to open up people's awareness to themselves because when it comes down to it, it's all about that; self-awareness. I'm just concerned that people don't party themselves back into slavery."[16]

The O'Jays recorded a Gamble and Huff number called "Ship Ahoy" (*Ship Ahoy*, Philadelphia K2–33150) that directs its masterful production to illustrating the ongoing evil impact of slavery on black Americans. The Temptations took over where The O'Jays left off with the clear and unambivalent "Message from a Black Man" (*The Temptations*, Motown Special STMX 6002, 1970). The song is a statement of defiance and intent to a racist society. Black people, it affirms, are no longer willing to be held back because of the color of their skin, and the deep dark voice of Denise Edwards warns that black freedom can no longer be denied.

In "Urban Warrior" (*Single Life*, 100 Club Phonogram JABH14, 1985) Cameo uses funk and rap, and a generous sprinkling of humor, to put down the rap artists and DJs who only play at being "urban warriors." In the following track on the same album, "Little Boys— Dangerous Toys," random violence is dismissed over a reggae beat, and it is suggested that people take responsibility for their own lives instead of attributing mugging and drug pushing to "society." Cameo comments effectively on almost every important area of life in *Word Up*. Sex and politics, poverty and wealth, change and stagnation are all viewed through sharply defined yet multifaceted musical prisms. Blues stands alongside hard rock, and hints of jazz dance around the pervasive funk. Cameo is success conscious enough to be aware that it appeals to those yuppies and buppies (young upwardly mobile people of both races) whose main aim is to acquire wealth and status. Yet it is retaining autonomy over its productions, its record company, and most importantly, its ideas. Cameo writes wry, outrageous, questioning lyrics over funky, staccato music that precludes smug acceptance of the existing pattern of American life as easy or comfortable for too many of its citizens.

Melle Mel is more obviously attacking the system when he raps with furious insight about the mess the United States, led by Reagan is in, and rants about poverty and nuclear power. He makes his attack positive by hanging on to hope of a better life if only people can come to their senses (*Beat Street—Original Soundtrack*, Atlantic 780154). This is music that could alter views and affect lifestyles. That is even more true of the newest single by the wonderboy of Minneapolis. When Prince put out "Sign of the Times" (*Sign of the Times*, Paisley Park/WEA WX 88C/925 577-4, 1987) in 1987, a shudderingly impressive song startled a lot of complacent people into a new sense of awareness. Nobody with any sensitivity could continue to ignore AIDS, drug abuse, poverty, deprivation, or the possibility of total world destruction through war. He is dealing with the kinds of problems that beset every country, and may raise consciousness about them enough to catalyze not just a shift in attitudes but a move to action.

The actively therapeutic value of music was emphasized by Bobby McFerrin in an interview with Jools Holland on "The Tube" in November 1986. He then said, "Basically we're all here to help one another, and music is a very potent and very healing force." In much the same way, both Lou Rawls and Billy Paul see music as a means of increasing black autonomy and self-respect.[17] Self-respect and drug taking are often viewed as mutually incompatible, and music has consistently been used to point out the dangers of drug abuse, from Gil Scott-Heron's "Angel Dust" (*Secrets*, Arista 4189) through Melle Mel's "White Lines" to the current spate of anti-crack songs like General Caine's "Crack Killed Apple Jack" (Motown, 1986).

If drugs provided a destructive and unacceptable form of escape, Africa shone on the horizon as a more positive haven for many black people in the "new world." There is no doubt that in a large number of Caribbean and British reggae records, the desire to "return" to Africa is a recurring theme. The Wailing Souls are among those who sing of Africa as their "homeland," and dream of real freedom and a sense of belonging once they are back in the land of their forefathers (*Inchpinchers*, Greensleeves GREL 47, 1983). Black Uhuru looks to Africa for sustenance and inspiration on "World is Africa" (*Black Uhuru*, Island IRG 13, 1985).

In the music that has emerged from Grenada, however, Africa is viewed less as an inspiration and more as a continent starving because of unjust exploitation. In the late 1970s and early 1980s in Grenada, revolution was promoted and encouraged through song. Calypsonians not only took a stand on the island's problems but also attacked those who spilled "innocent blood in El Salvador, innocent blood spill in Vietnam" and so many other inappropriate places.[18] They exhorted people to "listen to my song" and find strength in unity

> Because a people that is united
> No way at all could be defeated.[19]

Bob Marley had expressed a very similar view when he said, "You see, I believe it's music that brings people together."[20] He and The Wailers sang on "Top Rankin" (*Survival*, Island ILPS 9542, 1979):

> They don't want to see us write
> 'cause all they want us to do is
> keep on fussing and fighting
> they don't want to see us live together.

Bands have even been formed around the idea of unity. Unity is, in fact, the name of a group of black British musicians including "Lovers Rock" singer Caroll Thompson, Black Slate's former lead singer Keith Drummond, La Famille percussionist Lenny Edwards, and Alan Weekes, guitarist from the same band. They formed in 1983 to make a record called *People of the World* for the Bethnal Green Carousel label. Elroy Bailey, bassist and spokesman for Unity, explained, "We wanted to stress the point of unity, which is the answer to what we seek, a better world. The song 'People of the World' means unity, and the way we got the group together is an example of that."[21]

Aswad, the Ladbroke Grove British band, echoed these sentiments in 1982 when they said that their aim "was to bring over a message, to bring people together."[22] They also see politics as intrinsic to life and music, and understand that unity and harmony will not easily be won in societies based on policies of divide and rule.

It is very much in this spirit of joining together to combat exploitation and poverty that records have been made to fight for causes and raise funds simultaneously. Just as singles were cut to aid Ethiopia and South Africa, so musicians have gotten together to help combat a disease and a deprivation that affect black people. People in Progress made *This Is My Song* (Polydor, POSP 829, 1986) in aid of sickle-cell anemia research and the Canon Collins Educational Trust Fund for South Africa. The song, written by the black British group Imagination, blends gospel with funky rhythms to enhance the impact of the direct lyrics that attack both discrimination and disease.

In "Third World Revolution" Gil Scott-Heron stresses the intentions of black people all over the world to take control of their own lives and create a Third World revolution in which they can "take this world through changes, not the other way around."[23] He believes that songs can be instrumental in initiating those changes, and that music can sustain those who fight oppression. For centuries black people have stored their anger in song and have accompanied their battles for freedom with music. So long as inequality exists, the struggle will find strength and inspiration in music.

Bobby Womack not only writes "songs with a message that people can relate to," he also wants to organize an open-air picnic in Cleveland, his hometown. He plans to charge five dollars (including food), and take "the profits and personally go into the poor areas, knock on every door, and try to help out."[24] He wants to provide food and rent for the needy, and says if more bands did this, there would soon be no hunger.

But it is not charity that will really alleviate poverty and inequality. Freedom from need and freedom from discrimination can come about only through changes in the political and economic power structure in those countries that base their wealth on the exploitation of black and poor people. Singers are gaining the confidence and strength to pit their wits and voices against the forces of opppression with fresh determination and energy. Drawing inspiration from the past and with hope in the future, music is encouraging and aiding this dawning of a better day, a time when people are divided by neither economic exploitation nor the color of their skin.

NOTES

1. Ron Welburn, "The Black Aesthetic Imperative," in Addison Gayle, ed., *The Black Aesthetic* (New York: Doubleday, 1971), pp. 13, 135, 149.

2. William McClendon, "Black Music: Sound and Feeling for Liberation," *Black Scholar*, January–February 1976, pp. 20–21.

3. Interview with Bobby Bland by this author at Tipitina's, New Orleans, April 16, 1987.

4. Stephen de Grange, "Freedom New: The Temple That Max Roach Built," *Freedomways*, 21, no. 1 (1981): 41.

5. Interview with Abacush by this author at the Tropical Palace, Kensal Rise, London, December 17, 1983.

6. Interview: "Michael Smith 1954 to 1983," *Grassroots*, October/ November 1983, p. 4; Mark Kamba, "Rootsman Blues," *Black Echoes*, September 17, 1983, p. 6.

7. Carl Gayle, "I-Roy Was Here," *Black Music*, December 1973, p. 14.

8. John Collins, *African Pop Roots: The Inside Rhythms of Africa* (London: W. Foulsham & Co., 1985), p. 20.

9. Interview with Fela Kuti by this author at the Academy, Brixton, November 12, 1983.

10. Collins, *African Pop*, p. 45.

11. David B. Coplan, *In Township Tonight! South Africa's Black City Music and Theatre* (London: Longman, 1986), p. 246.

12. Coplan, *Township*, pp. 195–198.

13. Dave Harker, *One for the Money. Politics and Popular Song* (London: Hutchinson, 1980), p. 212.

14. Donald Byrd, "Music Without Aesthetics," *Black Scholar*, July–August 1978, p. 5.

15. Samuel Charters, sleeve notes for Son House and J. D. Short, *Delta Blues*, Transatlantic Records Xtra 1080.

16. "Ayers over Africa," *Blues and Soul* no. 300 (1973): 19.

17. Lou Rawls, *A Man of Value*, MGMSE-4861 (1972); Billy Paul, *Only the Strong Survive*, Philadelphia International 82236 (1977).

18. Polly E. McLean, "Calypso and Revolution in Grenada," *Popular Music and Society*, 10, no. 4 (1986): 92.

19. McLean, "Calypso," pp. 91, 97.

20. Quoted by Brant Newborn, "Marley Tribute Draws 20,000 to Montego Bay," *Rolling Stone*, October 1, 1981.

21. Penny Reel, "Collect and Survive," *New Musical Express*, March 5, 1983, p. 12.

22. Chris May, "Mustn't Give up Now," *Black Music and Jazz Review*, August 1982, p. 18.

23. Gil Scott-Heron and Brian Jackson, *Secrets*, Arista Spart 1073 (1978).

24. Interview on "The Tube," February 20, 1987, Channel 4, England.

Selected Bibliography

BOOKS

Bastin, Bruce. *Red River Blues: The Blues Tradition in the Southeast.* Basingstoke: Macmillan, 1986.

Bebey, Francis. *African Music: A People's Art.* New York: Lawrence Hill, 1975.

Bradford, Sarah. *Harriet Tubman: The Moses of Her People.* New York: Corinth, 1961.

Broven, John. *Walking to New Orleans: The Story of New Orleans Rhythm and Blues.* Bexhill-on-Sea, East Sussex: Flyright, 1977.

Chambers, Iain. *Urban Rhythms: Pop Music and Popular Culture.* London: Macmillan, 1985.

Clarke, Sebastian (Saba Saakana). *Jah Music: The Evolution of the Popular Jamaican Song.* London: Heinemann, 1980.

Collins, John. *African Pop Roots: The Inside Rhythms of Africa.* London: W. Foulsham & Co., 1985.

Coplan, David B. *In Township Tonight! South Africa's Black City Music and Theatre.* London: Longman, 1986.

Davis, Angela. *Women, Race and Class.* Shoreditch: Women's Press, 1981.

Dixon, Robert, and John Godrich. *Blues and Gospel Records, 1902–1942: A Discography.* London: Rust, 1969.

Epstein, Dena. *Sinful Tunes and Spirituals: Black Folk Music to the Civil War.* Urbana: University of Illinois Press, 1977.

Finn, Julio. *The Bluesman: The Musical Heritage of Black Men and Women in the Americas.* London: Quartet, 1986.

Frederikse, Julie. *South Africa: A Different Kind of War.* Gweru: Mambo Press, 1986.

Frith, Simon. *Sound Effects: Youth, Leisure and the Politics of Rock 'n' Roll*. London: Constable, 1983.

Gayle, Addison, ed. *The Black Aesthetic*. New York: Doubleday, 1971.

Gillett, Charlie. *Making Tracks: The Story of Atlantic Records*. London: Panther, 1975.

———. *The Sound of the City: The Rise of Rock and Roll*. London: Souvenir Press, 1983.

Haralmbos, Mike. *Right On: From Blues to Soul in Black America*. London: Eddison, 1974.

Harker, Dave. *One for the Money: Politics and Popular Song*. London: Hutchinson, 1980.

Haydon, Geoffrey, and Denis Marks, eds. *Repercussions: A Celebration of African American Music*. London: Century Publishing, 1985.

Hoare, Ian, Clive Anderson, Tony Cummings, and Simon Frith. *The Soul Book*. London: Methuen, 1975.

Johnson, H., and J. Pines. *Reggae: Deep Roots Music*. London: Proteus, 1982.

Jones, Hettie. *Big Star, Fallin' Mama: Five Women in Black Music*. New York: Viking Press, 1974.

Jones, Leroi (Amiri Baraka). *Blues People*. New York: William Morrow, 1963.

Lieb, Sarah. *Mother of the Blues: A Study of Ma Rainey*. Boston: University of Massachusetts Press, 1981.

Litwack, Leon. *Been in the Storm So Long: The Aftermath of Slavery*. London: Athlone Press, 1979.

Marable, Manning. *Race, Rebellion and Reform: The Second Reconstruction in Black America, 1945–1982*. London: Macmillan, 1984.

Marcus, Greil. *Mystery Train: Images of America in Rock 'n' Roll Music*. New York: Dutton, 1982.

Marre, Jeremy, and Hannah Carlton. *Beats of the Heart: Popular Music of the World*. London: Pluto, 1985.

Marsh, Dave. *Sun City by Artists Against Apartheid: The Making of the Record*. Harmondsworth: Penguin, 1985.

Newton, Huey. *Revolutionary Suicide*. London: Wildwood House, 1974.

Nicholas, A. X., ed. *Woke up This Morning: Poetry of the Blues*. New York: Bantam, 1973.

Oakley, Giles. *The Devil's Music: A History of the Blues*. London: British Broadcasting Corporation, 1976.

Oliver, Paul. *Blues Fell This Morning*. London: Cassell, 1959.

Stewart-Baxter, Derrick. *Ma Rainey and the Classic Blues Singers*. London: Studio Vista, 1970.

Street, John. *Rebel Music: The Politics of Popular Music*. Oxford: Basil Blackwell, 1986.

Troop, David. *The Rap Attack: African Jive to New York Hip Hop*. London: Pluto, 1984.

Wallace, Michele. *Black Macho and the Myth of Superman*. London: John Calder, 1979.

Webber, Thomas. *Deep like the Rivers*, New York: Norton, 1978.

Whitburn, Joel. *Top Rhythm and Blues Records, 1949–1971*. Menomonee Falls, WI: Record Research, 1974.

————. *The Billboard Book of U.S. Top 40 Hits, 1955 to Present*. Enfield: Guinness, 1983.

Wolfenstein, Eugene V. *The Victims of Democracy: Malcolm X and the Black Revolution*. Berkeley: University of California Press, 1981.

JOURNALS AND MAGAZINES

Afro-Beat
Black Echoes
Black Music and Jazz Review (absorbed by *Blues and Soul*)
Black Scholar
Blues Unlimited
Freedomways (has ceased publication)
Jazz Journal
Juke Blues
Melody Maker
Popular Music and Society
Rolling Stone

Index

About the Author

MARY ELLISON is senior lecturer in American studies at the University of Keele, England, where she runs programs in African-American history and culture for undergraduate and graduate students. She received her B.A. and Ph.D. from the University of London. Her publications include *The Black Experience, Extensions of the Blues,* and articles for *Phylon* and *Popular Music and Society.* Dr. Ellison's current research is on African-American history and music in New Orleans and Chicago.